ANGER MANAGEMENT FOR PARENTS

HOW TO BE CALMER AND MORE PATIENT WITH YOUR CHILDREN

KATHERINE GUZMAN

© **Copyright 2020 - All rights reserved.**

The content contained within this book may not be reproduced, duplicated or transmitted without direct written permission from the author or the publisher.

Under no circumstances will any blame or legal responsibility be held against the publisher, or author, for any damages, reparation, or monetary loss due to the information contained within this book, either directly or indirectly.

Legal Notice:

This book is copyright protected. It is only for personal use. You cannot amend, distribute, sell, use, quote or paraphrase any part, or the content within this book, without the consent of the author or publisher.

Disclaimer Notice:

Please note the information contained within this document is for educational and entertainment purposes only. All effort has been executed to present accurate, up to date, reliable, complete information. No warranties of any kind are declared or implied. Readers acknowledge that the author is not engaged in the rendering of legal, financial, medical or professional advice. The content within this book has been derived from various sources. Please consult a licensed professional before attempting any techniques outlined in this book.

By reading this document, the reader agrees that under no circumstances is the author responsible for any losses, direct or indirect, that are incurred as a result of the use of the information contained within this document, including, but not limited to, errors, omissions, or inaccuracies.

CONTENTS

Introduction   5

1. WHY DO WE GET ANGRY AS PARENTS?   13
   Potential Causes of Parental Anger   13

2. MANAGING ANGER TO BENEFIT ALL FACETS OF LIFE   22
   Anger Management Outside of the Parental Role   22

3. EMOTIONAL INTELLIGENCE   34
   What is Emotional Intelligence and How is it Beneficial   35

4. HANDLING PARENTAL ANGER WHEN IT DOES HAPPEN   42
   The Aftermath of Parental Anger   42

5. THE EFFECTS OF PARENTAL ANGER ON CHILDREN   50
   The Psychological Impact of Anger on Children   51

6. THE IMPORTANCE OF SELF-CARE AS A PARENT   59
   What is Self Care and How Can it Help Me?   59

7. PARENTING STYLES TO CONSIDER   71
   What are Parenting Styles   71

8. FINDING CALM THROUGH THE FIRST YEAR STORM   79
   Development and Triggers in The First Year   79

9. PATIENCE FOR THE TODDLER AND PRESCHOOL YEARS   88
Development Of Toddlers and Preschoolers   88

10. MANAGING ANGER WITH SCHOOL AGED KIDS   96
Development of School Aged Children   96

11. PATIENT PARENTING WITH TEENAGERS   103
Taking on the Teenage Years   103

Conclusion   111
References   117

INTRODUCTION

Parenting is undoubtedly one of the most complex, fulfilling, and challenging responsibilities many people will undertake throughout the course of their adult lives. Due to the pressure we feel to succeed as parents, it can be easy to allow our emotions to control the way we react to and handle the situations that make us feel angry or uncertain. Learning about our emotions, as well as those of our children, can help us develop a healthy approach to parenting and provide us with an opportunity to build a strong and lasting relationship with our children. Whether you are a seasoned expert, new to the parent's club, or soon-to-be embarking on your parenting journey, this eBook contains some valuable information for the inevitable hurdles you will face at various points throughout your child's life. Most people have some form of preconceived notions regarding what their parenting experience will look like. Some people who have fond memories of a considerably simple childhood with laid-back parents may expect they will have very little reason to discipline their own children. Having a child who expresses their emotions, positive or negative, differently than they did themselves can throw some parents a major curveball if they weren't prepared for this possibility. On the other hand, many among us may have told ourselves more than once, "I will never treat my own kids like this when I become a parent" due to trauma associated with what we considered unjust punishments, abusive households, negligent parenting, or any other myriad of reasons. Oftentimes, though, we may find ourselves repeating those exact behaviors which we swore we would never carry out, causing even more trauma to ourselves and, in turn, our children.

The way we are raised will often have a lasting impact on how we conduct ourselves as adults in general, and even more specifically on how we choose to raise our own children when the time comes. What many people don't realize when they first become a parent is that every child is, in fact, different. If you have multiple children already or if you had siblings when you were growing up, you are more likely to already be aware of this fact. Different children within the same family or household can still have very separate experiences and thus provide parents with a disparate set of obstacles than their siblings. Parents will often actually end up fine-tuning their parenting as they raise any additional children because they can better determine what worked or what had the opposite effect. This altered parenting approach can cause some siblings to accuse their parents of having a favorite as a result of them having a less rigid regime with the younger children in the family. While it can be frustrating for older children, being flexible and having the ability to adapt to this book's approach is a skill that will benefit both the parents and their children long term.

We are fortunate to be living in the 21st century, where information on a variety of subjects is readily available. Whereas, our parents and their parents relied only on what they knew personally and what they had been taught based on generations of child rearing before them. As a result of the strong sense of tradition attached to the parenting advice of our ancestors, there is often still a stigma around choosing to parent in what our families may consider an unorthodox way. Those of us who decide to seek out ways to better ourselves as people, as parents, and want to provide the best possible foundation for our children simply need to remember that it is a luxury our progenitors did not typically have. Taking time to research ways to better manage our emotions, and actively working with our children to develop these skills to manage their own, is a pragmatic approach to setting our children up for success as they become more independent.

As difficult as it is for parents to see their baby turn into a young adult in what seems to be the blink of an eye, it is also one of the most rewarding feelings. There is comfort in knowing that we have prepared our little ones to go out and face the world along with all of the emotional ups and downs they will experience for themselves as they set off on their own journeys. Building a strong bond and parent-child relationship can help us keep them close, no matter where their lives may take them. The cornerstone to forging that relationship is to do our best to provide the most loving, nurturing, and emotionally healthy childhood that we are able to. To accomplish this, we must not only keep our children's needs in mind, but we must also ensure we are taking care of ourselves. For some reason, people often dismiss the parents' needs and desires solely because they are parents. It can sometimes feel as if choosing to raise a child and love them with your whole heart means you cannot possibly have any room in that same heart for passion toward anything else. This widely held belief is partly to blame for causing so many of us parents to end up feeling guilty, overwhelmed, angry, impatient, and far from calm. In this eBook, we will cover some of the developmental stages of our children, the impact of their emotional and mental development on their behavior, and how we can adapt our parenting style to best fit within that unique dynamic.

There is no one-size-fits-all solution to parenting, and there is no secret to prevent us from occasionally acting out on our emotionally driven impulses. Sometimes we will get angry, sad, frustrated, or disappointed, and some of those instances may end with a negative response that we wanted so badly to avoid. When those failures do happen, it is important to remind ourselves that we are human, and we are indeed fallible. Teaching our children to navigate these complicated feelings can help us to overcome our own struggles by taking responsibility for our actions and demonstrating that it is ok to fail sometimes. It gives us the chance to improve and learn from our mistakes, a skill our children will need when they have to face challenges on their own. Taking the initiative to explore some specific techniques for parenting that we may not have otherwise considered has the potential to further reduce the instances of anger or impatience as we move through our parenting journey. Understanding our own emotional intelligence and applying that to the interactions we have with our children is also discussed later on and can help you to become more aware of your feelings and how they can impact the decisions you make. Knowing some of the things that may be triggers for you is beneficial when it comes to handling a fussy baby, reasoning with an emotionally immature toddler, and it can even help to calmly navigate the ever-changing moods of a teenager.

The suggestions and advice in this eBook are not only applicable to parenting; learning how to better manage your anger and remain calm will have results that carry over into other aspects of life. There are practical reasons to make an effort to become more emotionally healthy overall. It can enhance our relationships with our spouses, partners, friends, and extended family. All of us have become angry or frustrated to the point of losing control of our emotions and reacting in a way that leaves us feeling ashamed and full of regret. Being able to avoid that type of negative response can be much less taxing on our mental health and our ability to work through conflicts that arise. There are different types of anger, which we will explore later on, and there will certainly be times when we feel it is justifiable to raise our voice to express how someone has made us feel. We can seek to improve our application of emotional intelligence in these situations to help keep a level-head and enable us to better communicate how we are feeling. The goal of this eBook is to find the approach that works best for each person and their unique family dynamic. The aim is to help parents gain a better understanding of why we experience the emotional turmoil we do and why we sometimes get so angry with our children. Tackling our emotions can be a sensitive subject for some people, especially when it comes down to the possible causation of their anger being rooted in their own childhood experiences. There is no right or wrong way to seek help in becoming a more emotionally healthy person and a more patient parent. This is a stepping stone to becoming the parent you want to be, and in choosing to do so, you have already taken the first step to managing your anger and emotions for a more peaceful, calm, and well-balanced life.

1

WHY DO WE GET ANGRY AS PARENTS?

POTENTIAL CAUSES OF PARENTAL ANGER

When we set out on our journey as parents, there are often some expectations we have in terms of how our children will progress and learn, as well as expectations for ourselves as their parents. In most cases, the actual experiences we have in child-rearing will be altogether different than anything we had anticipated. What complicates our early attempts to posit how our new chapter will play out is other parents' stories in our social and familial circles. It is safe to assume that most people know someone who took it upon themselves to share their own idyllic anecdotes of parenting, and it just so happened to be on a day when our own children had pushed every button, and we just wanted to have someone tell us our emotions were normal. I am talking about the usually well-intentioned friends and family who regale us with stories of their perfectly behaved and easily adaptable newborns, their toddlers who are ahead of all their peers at daycare, or their school-aged kids who don't have a defiant bone in their bodies. It is important to remember, though, that these stories are most likely embellished at least in part, and they are exposing only the best aspects of their family life, which is fine, and it is entirely up to them to disclose what they so choose. It does, however, make it even more challenging for many parents to determine what they should expect from their own children. Hearing stories from people who have seemingly perfect children can make parents question their abilities in raising their own and cause them to wonder if they may be at the root of any issues they are having.

One way to reduce the anger or frustration we feel, as parents, is by forming realistic ideas of what we expect our children to accomplish, when they should do so, and how we believe they should act and feel. There is obviously a lot of pressure to make sure our children reach all of the same developmental milestones as their siblings or other children we interact with. It sometimes feels like a competition among parents to have the child who met these goals ahead of the curve. This can lead to toxic situations in which parents are adding undue stress to the lives of themselves and their children when, in reality, every child is different and develops at their own pace. It can become problematic if we try to adhere too closely to arbitrary timelines for our children's development. For example, if they don't say their first word by ten months old, we might worry that we have already set them up for failure and need to get them into speech therapy immediately. Of course, this is absolutely not the case. Putting this kind of pressure on ourselves will only cause emotional strain and open the door to potentially becoming angry and frustrated when we don't see the progress we had expected.

Fear of failure is something most people struggle with in their everyday lives, so when it comes to the fear that we may be failing as a parent, that is when the stakes become even higher, and our negative emotions can overtake our logic. Consulting the internet can very easily lead parents down a path of misinformation, generalization, and assumptions regarding their child's behavior. The sense that we may be failing our children is exacerbated when we start to see terms such as "developmental delay" or "reduced cognitive ability." This is not to say that children who may have any type of developmental delay or mental illness are failures in any way whatsoever; it is just something that can send up red flags and set off alarms in the minds of parents who are already emotionally charged and angry with themselves. If this can all be avoided by managing our expectations before they cause us to become angry or impatient, we can work with our children to provide the tools they need to learn and develop in their own time.

There are times when we will become angry with our children for less obvious reasons and inadvertently draw on our own childhood experiences. We may have learned certain behaviors and reactions from our own parents or caregivers, and subconsciously incorporated them into our approach as we raise our own children. This is a perfect example of how it can be beneficial to take some time to research and learn more about other ways to handle parenting, different techniques to try, and ultimately what options we have to parent the best way for our family. Following the same methods that were used by our own parents, whether or not we do so intentionally, is a common practice and can lead to us mirroring anger based reactions to the challenges we face with our children. Taking the time to contemplate why we are reacting angrily to our children can help determine whether or not this is due in part to what researchers have often referred to as "ghosts in the nursery." When we become parents, the emotions and experiences of our own childhood can be revived, and if we don't take the time to reflect on how we felt as a child, or if perhaps we don't have the best recall of that time in our lives, we can allow these ghosts to return and haunt us. If we have memories of being yelled at and punished for not eating everything on our plates during mealtimes, then it may end up feeling like an appropriate response to our young child not wanting to eat the serving we provided them. An alternative way we could approach this is to explain that it is ok if they do not want to finish their meal; however, there will not be extra snacks offered and that the only option, if they are hungry later, would be to finish what had been served previously. This type of response empowers our children to make their own choices while understanding the repercussions as well as developing a better understanding of their own eating habits and relationship with food. Turning situations where our initial reaction may have been anger or frustration into opportunities for productive discourse and teaching important lessons can help us manage anger toward our children as well.

It is our job to educate our children on all aspects of being a well-rounded individual as they become more independent and interact with the world around them. Choosing this approach instead of defaulting to the ghosts of our own childhood can help show them that they are still people, even at a young age, and that they are able to make some decisions for themselves as long as they are willing to accept the consequences. This is only one example of how our childhood experiences or traumas can influence the way we go about parenting our own children, and there are many different situations and applications of this concept. We can begin to untangle the influence of our memories from our true intentions by being introspective and becoming aware of the things we may have simply accepted as being the only option. It is a natural response to follow in the footsteps of our own parents. It is not something that should be seen as a failure for those who had a less-than-perfect childhood, nor is it inherently a failure on the part of our own parents if we do choose to follow a different path.

A philosophy in which I firmly believe as a parent myself is that if we know better, then we can then do better. Things have absolutely changed since most of us were children ourselves; there is an abundance of new research into the psychological effect that different parenting styles can have on children. Historically it has been generally accepted that children were not to be given independence or flexibility by their parents, and it was very much a belief that parents were to be shown respect and obedience at all times under every circumstance. Now that we know more about nurturing our children, we are also beginning to understand that they will typically respond much better to a gentle approach rather than an angry one. We are able to apply this new information to our lives and our roles as parents in the hopes of doing better for our children than generations before us may have done.

Our Emotions and Triggers

Having a better understanding of what underlying emotions may actually be at the root of our angry responses can help us to become aware of the instances where we may direct those angry reactions toward our child, making it possible for us to head them off. It is generally uncomfortable to explore our anger and negative emotions; they tend to occur when we become heated, afraid, uncomfortable, or vulnerable, and that list just goes on. When we experience undesirable feelings, it is usually a situation where things have progressed quickly, and we are suddenly being presented with something we do not like, whatever it may be. Figuring out the "why" behind these experiences is the key to being able to actively decide not to allow our emotions to take control and leaving us regretting our actions later on. Prevention is the goal when it comes to understanding our triggers, and it is worth the effort to push through the negative associations and difficulties we may have to face them head-on.

As mentioned previously, everyone has their own unique experiences in life, and those experiences will almost always have a lasting impact on the way we interact with the world around us. If children come from a home that was often the scene of screaming matches, physical violence, and being told "no" all the time, it is likely that those behaviors will become triggers for them as adults.. If someone was always being called names and berated as a child and then having a child of your own who resorts to name-calling, as innocent as it may be, could be a major trigger for that parent's anger. When we are presented with these triggers, we are given a small window to process the situation and react. To learn to manage our anger, we must learn to take the high road in these situations; we must actively choose to use our emotional intelligence to control our mind and body before reaching the point of no return and lashing out at our children. Triggers are things that have become our weak points, our vulnerabilities, and in many cases, are the justifications we may use for our anger. If we can regain our composure when we feel triggered, then we stand a much better chance of calming down and engaging with our children in a meaningful and productive way.

Throughout our lives (and throughout this eBook), we often refer to negative emotions as anger. In reality, there are a number of emotions that cause us to appear angry; just being unsure of why we are feeling a certain way can lead to anger and a short-temper. Analyzing the events that lead up to our perceived anger can help us better identify the genuine emotion we are feeling. We can easily mistake any less-desirable feeling for anger. We may be feeling frustrated with our children because they just don't seem to understand what we are asking of them, we may be disappointed because they don't seem to appreciate the hard work we put into getting them what they want, or we may simply be feeling overwhelmed in other areas of our lives, and it is carrying over into the relationship with our children. When we become emotional and feel like we may be on the verge of losing our temper, that is the perfect time to take a deep breath and ask yourself what happened leading up to this moment. Try to figure out if you are actually angry with your child for a valid reason or if you are possibly feeling tired from a long day at work dealing with a difficult co-worker. Maybe you feel frustrated because you tried a new recipe, and it didn't turn out the way you wanted it to. Being a parent does not mean that we are no longer human. We continue to experience the full spectrum of emotions, and the best we can do is to try and develop healthy coping mechanisms to create the most positive environment for our children to learn about and express their own emotions.

If we learn the skills to manage our anger and take the time to consider what may be behind it, then we can offer these techniques to our children as they are developing their own sense of self-awareness. The most important thing to remember is that anger can come from many places, and finding the root can help us actively take back control of a situation. In doing so, we are also demonstrating this behavior for our children.

2

MANAGING ANGER TO BENEFIT ALL FACETS OF LIFE

ANGER MANAGEMENT OUTSIDE OF THE PARENTAL ROLE

People can often lose themselves in the seemingly endless to-dos of parenthood. If it isn't naps, preparing meals for the family, and household chores, then it's packing your children into the car and taking on the Saturday afternoon grocery store crowds. The demands of being a parent never really end. You might get some rest once in a while as they get older, but then you don't seem to know what to actually do with your free time. Amidst all the pressures and sleepless nights that come with being a parent, it is easy to forget we are people outside of that role. Parents are still individuals with interests, hobbies, often holding other jobs and careers and all while trying to maintain relationships with people other than our children. It is no secret that being a parent will have an impact one way or another on the connections we have with our partner or spouse. Obviously, not everyone will face serious issues within these relationships, but the added stress can cause friction where there was none before. This is also true of our relationships with friends, coworkers, employers, and even extended family members we are typically close to, like our own parents and siblings.

Whether it is a case of old friends feeling like we don't have time for them anymore, family members providing unsolicited advice, or maybe a coworker who points out that you missed a day of work due to a sick child in the hopes of securing favor with the boss. These situations are something most of us will have experienced at some point. Even if it was not specifically one of those examples, I'm sure there have been many times in life you have become angry as a person and not as a parent. It can seem less important that we try to control our anger when we are dealing with other adults; after all, they aren't children and should already know not to do things that may upset others.

We see examples of this all the time in everyday scenarios. If we don't know how to manage our own emotions and anger, then we may also simply accept these responses as normal or acceptable because they are among adults who we assume are emotionally aware enough to conduct themselves appropriately. An example of a time when we will benefit greatly from controlling our anger outside of being a parent would be to remember when you have been stuck in traffic, aggravated but keeping your cool as you see the vehicles ahead starting to move. Out of nowhere, a driver aggressively inches their way into the small space ahead of you, and you are now left with no choice but to allow this person to cut in front of you. Trying to accept the situation and move on, you allow them to pull in front as traffic continues to move forward. Then you watch, in what feels like slow motion, as that same car gets too close to yours, and you feel the impact as it scrapes your bumper. The anger starts to boil over at this point as you were already annoyed and frustrated before this incident, and from the looks of it, the other driver doesn't intend to get out of their car and check the damage they've just caused. I have personally seen this scenario play out in a couple of different ways, and one is typically much safer and emotionally sound than the other.

The first option we have is to give them the benefit of the doubt. Maybe they plan to get out and speak to you once they can clear the way and pull their car off to the side of the road. Maybe this person has good intentions and just wants to make sure the two of you are able to assess the damage while discussing the situation calmly. If we can effectively manage our anger despite the emotions we are dealing with in the heat of things, we will be much more likely to come to a resolution safely and within just a few short minutes. The second option we have is to completely give in to the anger and the overwhelming feelings that have us reeling as we try to wrap our mind around why someone would do something so careless, especially after *we* were kind enough to tolerate their aggressive lane change prior to the accident. The route we take here will set the tone for the interaction we are about to have with the other driver. While we are making these choices in our own vehicle, the other driver is doing the same. If both parties are ready to come out and peacefully handle the situation, everyone is going to leave feeling much more collected and at ease. If one or both drivers decide to let their anger take over, reason and diplomacy will go out the window, causing things to go from bad to worse pretty quickly. These driving-related emotional surges are commonly known as road rage, and they are not related to being a parent, but they are present in our society and could be altogether avoided if people learned how to control the waves of emotion when they are faced with uncertainty and in some cases, justifiable anger.

As mentioned, I have seen this type of altercation go both ways. The angry, aggressive drivers are almost always too emotional to make any progress with the other party. They may even cross lines that put them on the wrong side of the law, regardless of the fact that they were the victim of the other driver's negligence. Taking a calm approach during these types of interactions will enable us to take note of the other person's information and listen to their side of things. Ultimately we just want to be grateful and appreciate the fact that no one was injured (hopefully) and that we were afforded the luxury of even deciding whether or not to be angry. This is one application of anger management that is pretty commonplace. If you have ever been in the shoes of either driver, I am certain you appreciated it if the other party conducted themselves in a calm, patient manner rather than getting irate or, even worse, becoming physical.

Learning how to better communicate in situations that cause us to feel angry and uncomfortable can be extremely practical. For example, it is obviously not recommended that we express how angry we are with a boss or close friend immediately following a triggering situation. We learned what triggers are in the previous chapter, and it is important to note that anyone, not just our children, can activate them. We can become triggered by anyone in our lives who happens to say or do the right things to set us off and does so at the wrong time. If we can learn how to recognize the things that have the potential to create a volatile situation, we are going to be much better equipped to react more calmly.

In some cases, this may mean we need to walk away from a situation and take some time to process the experience. This might just be to do some breathing exercises, or it could mean taking some extra time to cool-down so that we can allow our anger to run its course before returning to handle things with a clear mind. Giving ourselves an adult version of a "time-out" when we are angry can be extremely effective and allows us the time to consider our options and how we wish to proceed.

I am sure everyone reading this has, at some point, reacted in anger to someone in their life and, in hindsight, realized that they felt silly or wished they could go back and do things differently using a much different approach. When we are in the heat of the moment and become irate due to a number of underlying feelings and thoughts, we can do things that we feel ashamed of when we have had that downtime to reflect on everything that took place. At the end of the day, no one enjoys blowing up over the little things in life, and we all know that the time we spend angry is time we don't get back. While it won't work every time, trying to take that step back to determine if the situation warrants an angry response can have a major impact on our ability to control these impulses and direct our energy to more productive methods of conflict resolution. In order to begin to manage our anger and emotions more proactively, it is helpful to understand a bit more about some of the different types of anger that there are, how we might express them, and how the anger of others can impact our ability to stay calm when faced with an uncomfortable confrontation.

Different Types of Anger

As you are beginning to see, anger is a very complex emotion. There can be many contributing factors and related emotions that cause us to act out angrily when, in reality, we are feeling insecure, fearful, uncomfortable, annoyed, etc. When we are trying to gain control of the way we express ourselves and communicate, we want to try and address the specific emotions we are experiencing. It will be much easier to explain our perspective to someone else if we can share more than just the fact that we are angry or upset. In situations with close personal relationships, our anger will often stem from being hurt or feeling insecure. Instead of getting angry at our partners for something they said or did that may seem to be blatantly insensitive to us, we are much better served to explain why it affected us the way it did and how we perceived their role in the quarrel. Being able to provide insight into our emotions and being open to understanding those of the other party can help us avoid either side blowing things out of proportion. This practice is similarly applicable to those times we may have a disagreement in the workplace. If we can remain calm, diplomatic, and professional while still expressing how we feel about a situation, we are much more likely to come to a favorable resolution. If we make the effort to learn how our coworker feels, we can work together to improve productivity and avoid future power struggles or miscommunications.

At the very least, when we take the time to listen to our partners, friends, families, coworkers, and even our children, we get the chance to analyze the whole situation and not just from our standpoint. This can help how we choose to interact with these people in the future and in gauging triggering situations better. Some people will be able to make us angry and push our buttons better and more frequently than others, but knowing when we need to take action before we become angry is beneficial to all those involved. In order to better judge the situations in which we may have to decide it's not worth our time and energy, we need to understand the different types of anger we may feel or may receive from those with whom we engage.

We have all felt the need to utter a snarky comment or leave a note for a spouse or roommate who just doesn't seem to understand how to get dishes from the sink to the dishwasher. These annoyances and pet peeves that we all have can contribute to passive-aggressive anger. This is a type of anger that is quite common but can lead to more direct and problematic aggressive displays of anger if left unchecked. Many people don't see much harm in their tendency to be passive-aggressive, and it feels more acceptable because it isn't really a confrontational display of anger, and it doesn't often cause much harm. However, it can add up, taking a toll on both the perpetrator and the victim of the passive-aggressive attacks. If we get into a disagreement with a coworker, we may decide we have to print 300 copies of a form despite the fact that we just overheard them saying they needed to print some important time-sensitive documents. Rushing to the printer and giving them a smirk and a shrug as they return to their desk in a huff is passive-aggressive and could understandably lead to a complicated working relationship with that person in the future. Just because there was no all-out dispute in the office that day does not mean that there will not be consequences down the road or that others didn't pick up on the passive-aggression. Other examples of some ways in which people may be passive-aggressive are:

- acting as if they are a victim of the other person and as if they have done nothing wrong
- making snide remarks in the presence of, or to acquaintances of, the other person
- purposely not completing tasks they were asked to do despite knowing the importance of them
- purposely being 'too busy' to address issues or communicate to solve problems

- being misleading in the communication they do have with others
- being sarcastic and possibly not being very clear that was the intention

There are plenty of different ways people can be passive-aggressive, and it will often leave people feeling confused, belittled, and angry themselves. The best way to handle someone who is being passive-aggressive is to confront them head-on because this kind of behavior is fueled by a lack of direct confrontation. If it is addressed directly, it will often leave little room for further manipulation and force both parties to deal with the friction.

On the opposite end of the spectrum is open aggression. This is anger that is shown outright; this type of anger is not lowkey and does not attempt to avoid confrontation. If someone is openly aggressive, they will likely appear irate. One of the characteristics of open aggression is becoming abusive, which may be in the form of emotional and verbal abuse when people resort to yelling, name-calling, and generally berating their victim. In some cases, people who are openly aggressive will act out physically; they can use their overwhelming flood of emotions to inflict pain and harm on others who they feel have mistreated them. This type of anger can sometimes be confused by those who experience it for justifiable anger, but that is not necessarily the case. Justifiable anger occurs when there truly is a reason for someone to feel anger in response to a certain situation. The way we often gauge whether or not anger is justifiable is through the way others subjectively view the situation. There are often times we will hear about someone who has acted out in a display of open aggression and find ourselves agreeing with their actions. In cases we see on the news regarding abused women who injured or killed their abuser, many people find it easier to accept her actions, while still illegal, as being carried out due to justifiable anger. The same may be said for someone who sees an act of animal abuse being committed and takes it upon themselves to physically assault the abuser and detain them until authorities arrive. These actions are still considered criminal, but the reason they were committed is a result of actions society deems unacceptable, to begin with. These circumstances are often considered in court cases when someone is being charged with a crime, and the defense lawyers attempt to explain that there was justification for their client's actions. It might not always result in the accused being found not guilty, but there is a chance for a lesser punishment due to these mitigating factors.

The final type of anger we will cover is assertive anger, and it is a considerably better way to try and express our anger if at all possible. Being assertive with our emotions is one of the things that we are striving for throughout the whole process of learning how to manage our anger and be calmer. When we have learned how to regain control of our anger, we are then able to be assertive. Having the ability to explain how we are feeling and the willingness to listen to input from others can keep us from escalating situations and having to live with regrets later on. We are human, and this is not always going to be our initial response, but we can always change course and make an effort to give ourselves that time to step back, breathe, organize our thoughts and return to the situation with an open mind and a less aggressive demeanor. Everything in this chapter is applicable to our lives as parents, but we must also remember that while we are aiming to provide the best life for our children, we must take care of ourselves as well. Displacing anger that we feel toward someone or something else can be damaging to our children and outside relationships. Being mindful of how we feel and how we can best manage our anger is going to help every facet of life and provide our children with an emotionally healthier, well-rounded parent.

EMOTIONAL INTELLIGENCE

Becoming aware of our emotions and how they impact us is a big part of managing our reactions as parents and in general. Being emotionally intelligent allows us to empathize with our children and helps us control the situation to achieve a positive outcome rather than leaving both parent and child feeling unfulfilled. Emotional intelligence allows us to pinpoint our strengths and weaknesses more accurately, helping us become more in tune with our emotions. Developing these skills can further our ability as parents to set good examples for our children when dealing with emotionally charged situations in life. Some of the benefits of becoming more emotionally intelligent are:

- not holding onto conflicts after they have been dealt with

- not taking things to heart when there is no ill intent
- not allowing our choices to be controlled by negative emotions
- addressing mistakes made by either the parent or the child
- accepting responsibility for our actions.

Some people are naturally more emotionally intelligent than others, but that does not mean those who may struggle with this are doomed to perpetually trying to overcome obstacles imposed by a lower emotional quotient. There are some techniques and skills that we can apply to develop our ability to decode how we are feeling and better respond to situations based on specific emotions and triggers.

WHAT IS EMOTIONAL INTELLIGENCE AND HOW IS IT BENEFICIAL

When we use the term emotional intelligence or emotional quotient (EQ) as it is sometimes referred, we are talking about a few different aspects of our interpersonal communication skill set. The first part of our EQ is the level of awareness we have in terms of our own emotions. Simply put, this is how well we can identify and understand what we are feeling and why. People who may struggle with this would typically have a harder time deciphering why they feel anxious, angry, sad, or stressed. They would often just experience general emotional distress, causing them to be influenced by those feelings and make illogical, rash decisions. Alternatively, those who are able to more accurately identify the specific emotions they are feeling can then better use this information to consider their next steps and how to tackle the issues they are facing. That is the second part of what we consider EQ, the ability to apply our understanding of self to our actions. The last relevant section is combining the two previous skills and actively managing the emotions we are experiencing. Once we have identified the root of our anger and determined how we want to proceed, we are able to modulate our feelings and navigate complex interactions with others.

The goal of using emotional intelligence, or developing it, is to use our emotions to attain positive outcomes instead of becoming overwhelmed and reactive. There are countless applications of EQ in our lives that will help us build relationships and maintain the ones we have. As a parent, you can be more empathetic with your children if you are able to understand how you feel, how your child is feeling, and how to move forward together to reach a reasonable conclusion in any given situation. This is true of the interactions we have with others as well. Having a higher EQ will allow us to communicate better in social situations and benefit the different connections we make with others. It is not only going to help in terms of our ability to communicate; there is also an impact on our ability to manage stress, and, in turn, the physical side effects that come along with it. When we become stressed and are not appropriately managing it, we can see many different issues that arise with our physical health. It is generally accepted that those who live high-stress lives and work in stressful careers, for example, suffer heart attacks, strokes, and issues with blood pressure, among other ailments. If we are managing the emotions that contribute to our stress and are taking steps to channel how we are feeling into more productive activities, we can begin to feel better mentally and physically. Having comprehensive control of our emotional health is a major tool when it comes to anger management. If this is not something that you feel confident with, there are some techniques to use to improve your own emotional quotient; it is never too late to learn how to be self-examining. The emotions we feel are complicated, and it can take some time to become comfortable gauging how and why we may feel a certain way, but once we begin to augment this skill, we will see improvements in the ways we engage with our children.

Developing Emotional Intelligence for Parents and Children

When we first start working on our EQ, we will need to actively take certain steps when we are feeling angry or emotional so we can isolate and analyze how we are feeling. As we do this more frequently, the need to consciously break down every emotion will lessen, and we will have a naturally flowing system that works for us. Below are a few quick suggestions regarding how to approach your emotions to gain control and use them to your benefit:

- Take control of your emotions. When you feel yourself becoming angry, upset, frustrated, etc. decide to take back control. Pay close attention to the way you are feeling and how you are reacting in triggering situations. Consider the emotion you are feeling to be more than just a momentary sensation and try to dissect it for a better understanding of where it came from and what exactly it is. Make an effort to describe how you feel physically and mentally. If it helps to write these things down, a journal can be a great tool.
- Be aware of your body language when you become emotional. Many people will give off subtle clues as to how they are feeling using their body positioning and facial expressions. Crossing our arms, furrowing a brow, taking an aggressive stance, or turning our bodies away from others are

all some potential signs we may exhibit. Other physical manifestations of emotion are things like shaking, nausea, sweating, and even a sudden need to use the toilet. Our bodies are designed to help us defend ourselves against potential threats, and when we become emotional, our brains can send off internal signals to try and help us handle those situations.

- Take the time necessary to relax and center yourself. It might mean taking just a moment to step away to breathe and collect your thoughts, or you may need a bit longer to guide yourself through practicing the previous steps. Whatever feels right for you is the approach you should take. There is no right or wrong way to become more in-tune with yourself.

- One thing that many people do is shut down their emotions completely, and in doing so, they assume that there is no need to pay mind to the way they felt before closing themselves off. In order to effectively become emotionally aware and gain insight to benefit our lives, we have to allow the emotions to run their course. We first have to become comfortable experiencing our emotions so that we are then able to analyze them. The goal is to use our emotions positively even if it may be unpleasant in the beginning, the end result is well worth it.

- When it comes to helping our children with their own emotions, we would simply use the steps above. Without pressuring our child, we want to help them put a label on or give a name to the emotion they are experiencing. They may be angry that they don't get to eat another candy bar or sad because they have to come inside from playing with friends. Being able to address these feelings regardless of what they may be will help our children explore why they happen and encourages them to develop a skill they can use throughout their lives.

- By practicing our own emotional management, we are modeling this essential skill for our children. Seeing their parents take steps to handle overwhelming feelings, especially if we explain what we are doing and why can be a key to helping our children feel comfortable doing the same when they face those big feelings they don't quite understand.

- Finally, we want to embolden our children to experience their emotions, no matter how difficult it may be. As a parent, we have a duty to our children to prepare them as best we can to go out and face the world. There are times it is unavoidable to feel negative emotions, and we want to acknowledge how our child is feeling while walking them through identifying and accepting their emotions. It is never helpful to diminish their feelings or brush them off by saying things could be worse, let it go, or telling them to stop being babies. Everything we feel is valid because it is our truth, and whether we can relate to how our child is feeling or not, we cannot tell them how they feel.

Of course, the development of a healthy emotional awareness is something that takes time and practice, but we can help set our children up for success by demonstrating our own emotional intelligence. Whether it is something you developed naturally or you are one of the people who had to take some extra time to work on it, you are providing the model for your children to build on and carry with them throughout their life.

4

HANDLING PARENTAL ANGER WHEN IT DOES HAPPEN

THE AFTERMATH OF PARENTAL ANGER

Despite our best efforts and the time spent developing our emotional intelligence, there will still be times throughout our parenting journey when we will become angry. We are all only human, which means we are not perfect, nor should we try to present ourselves as perfect to our children. There is often a point in every young person's life when they realize that their parents are, in fact, fallible. How we choose to navigate our anger and emotions with our children can influence how they come to this conclusion. In some cases, children reach the age where they understand how to better manage their own emotions, and when they witness their parents' failure to do the same, it leads to the changed view of their parents. Children commonly place their parents up on a pedestal, and the revelation that they are not the flawless people they thought they were can be devastating for some. As parents, we can take control and avoid this type of outcome simply by proactively modeling how to handle the consequences of our anger. We have the ability to teach our children that regardless of whether or not our anger was justifiable, we can still apologize for the way we handled the situation and commit to working with our child (or whoever the other party may be) to communicate more effectively in the future. There is no shame in admitting that we could have acted differently when facing the challenges of parenting. The only time we are failing is if we allow our children to accept that angry, abusive, and overall negative reactions are the norm.

Part of the previous chapter explained that our aim is to choose assertive anger whenever possible and to channel that anger into a positive outcome. That does not mean that we can never get angry or make mistakes; it just means we need to ensure we are doing what we can to remedy them after the fact. Helping our children expand their understanding of this concept is important as well. We want our children to feel comfortable enough to express their emotions and, when necessary, accept any consequences that come along with them. Having self-compassion and accepting responsibility for our undesirable actions as parents allows our children to practice compassion, among other things. They will also be able to relate to their own feelings of regret when they inevitably act out or find themselves unable to control their emotions.

One of the most common things I have heard people say when it comes to how their own parents handled parental anger is that they never heard their parents apologize for their explosive reactions even when they visibly felt bad about their behavior. Many parents will try to avoid the subject and even go so far as to offer bribes or special treats and outings as a means of apologizing without actually taking responsibility. While that kind of response can be effective with young children who don't necessarily have the best memory or attention span, it usually doesn't cut it once children are older and understand that our actions impact others. If a parent has become worn down, stressed out, or is just having a bad day and ends up taking that out on their child, they are usually aware of it. For example, if our child was supposed to have their room clean and we find it hasn't been done, we are justifiably going to become annoyed, frustrated, or even angry. However, the way we react to this situation can determine whether or not we may need to apologize and take responsibility for the way we conducted ourselves. Our children look to us for guidance, care, comfort, and love. If we respond to every little issue with angry outbursts, then we are at risk of altering the way our children interact with us in the future. We do not want to leave our children fearful of how we will react if they make a mistake or do something wrong in our eyes. It is expected that there will be many difficult situations throughout their childhood, and if we have set the standard that we expect perfection from our children, then they learn that we value their obedience over their trust and comfort. By creating this type of environment for our children, we are tainting their safe space in both their home and with us as their parents.

Moving Forward After Anger

One method of moving past our emotional mishaps as parents is to work on our ability to control our internal monologue. When we make mistakes, we often end up spiraling mentally and putting ourselves down for the way we handled things when we know there was a better option. In order to move on and make the situation better for ourselves and our children, we must actively correct our thinking and decide that we are going to learn from our mistakes. Allowing ourselves to show some self-compassion can go a long way in terms of asking for forgiveness from our children. People tend to spend a lot of time beating themselves up for things they can't change and replaying the scenario in their minds. This is a normal response, but it is not at all a productive one. It will be difficult at first, but forgiving yourself for the times when you act out in anger is the absolute key to developing a healthy balance between failure and progress. Part of having a good sense of emotional intelligence is the ability to let things go when they are not serving us in life. There is no need to dwell on undesirable behaviors when we literally have the option to just accept that it happened and move forward. Taking some time to analyze the situation and the emotions we experienced, as a result, will help us to choose a better approach when faced with similar obstacles in the future. After we have processed and analyzed our missteps, it is important to provide our child with an opportunity to discuss the interaction and how it made them feel. Our children need to see that we are open to hearing their input and that we are willing to find a better solution together. Taking the time to review the events that took place together and how each person could have handled things differently will help improve the communication with our children and let them know that we are always going to be willing to hear them out.

As we learn more about our emotions and our capacity to forgive the mistakes made by our children and ourselves, we are going to be better able to identify patterns in our behavior. Sometimes there may be a need to seek additional help through other means, and being able to recognize that we might need to take some extra steps to secure our mental health and emotional well-being is a display of a higher emotional quotient in itself. There is never a reason to be ashamed or embarrassed for deciding to do whatever it takes to get a better handle on our anger, and there are resources available to help meet those goals. If you are still struggling with controlling anger, or at the very least being able to acknowledge it after the fact, then there may be some other things you can try on your own to help with improving your general state of mind.

We already know that reducing stress will prepare us to better manage our anger when it happens, so if we can find some positive activities that help us be more relaxed and calm, we are likely to reduce uncontrollable anger. As with any other habit we try to form, it will be necessary to consciously remind ourselves of our goal and push ourselves to repeat the new activity until we become more confident. Yoga and meditation are two common lifestyle changes that people take on in order to reduce their stress levels and live a more peaceful life. The great thing about living in the 21st century is the ability to find endless sources of information online. If you have access to the internet, you can easily find thousands of free resources for yoga and meditation. Watching videos and reading various blogs and forums can assist you on your path to learning how to begin and how to develop your skills. If online learning isn't working for you, you can always reach out to local businesses that provide yoga lessons and similar services. Oftentimes the first class is free and will help you gauge whether or not it is something you wish to pursue. If you are not the type of person who can incorporate that kind of lifestyle change into your daily routine, you may benefit from something a little different. Speaking to a counselor or therapist can provide some much needed insight and guidance into how we can manage difficult emotions and regain control in all areas of our lives. Having someone to guide you through the analysis of your anger and help you determine what might be causing things to get out of control can be the missing link for many people. There are misconceptions that those who seek therapy are weak-minded or lacking in some way, but this is absolutely not the case. Choosing to speak with someone who is an expert in how the human brain works and how we perceive different situations is the logical step for anyone who may be struggling to understand themselves.

Finally, if you are looking for a more specific and targeted type of guidance when it comes to tacklings issues with anger, there are also therapy groups that specialize in anger management. These types of courses typically cover more in-depth processes and techniques that will help manage more serious anger issues. Moving forward from anger is something we can always be working on and trying to improve. There will never be a point where we can say we have reached perfection and have complete control over our emotions or our anger. Using the skills and techniques in this eBook in a way that fits your life and unique circumstances is the true objective. No matter what combination of suggestions or resources you need to use to get there, the dedication to doing so is already progress and something to be extremely proud of. Sharing the things we learn with our children is also proactively helping them as they are becoming increasingly independent and emotionally intelligent themselves.

THE EFFECTS OF PARENTAL ANGER ON CHILDREN

One of the biggest motivators for many parents who want to better manage their anger and other emotions is knowing that their actions will have an impact on their children in multiple ways. There are some people, however, who come from a background of familial anger and emotional mismanagement. They may not have considered that their anger could have a far-reaching and long-lasting impact on their children. This goes back to the point mentioned in an earlier segment of this eBook that introduced the parenting philosophy of knowing better and doing better. Now that we have begun to understand that anger is not the best or healthiest approach to parenting or life in general, we know better and are able to apply that knowledge to the development of a new course of action. For some of us, anger was the normal reaction to disobedience or what was seen by our parents as a failure to meet their expectations in some way. While it is not uncommon to have had this experience as a child, it does not make it excusable. Most of the people who have memories of being yelled at, physically reprimanded, and being disciplined from a place of anger will have some negative emotions tied to that time with their parents. We have the opportunity to not only provide our children with a better experience than we had ourselves but to also work through some of the trauma that may have been inflicted upon us by regaining control of our own emotions.

THE PSYCHOLOGICAL IMPACT OF ANGER ON CHILDREN

We have established that the behavior we demonstrate for our children will heavily influence the way they act when they are interacting with peers and others throughout their lives. This is an extremely important point to keep in mind as we work on how we handle situations that call for more maturity and restraint on our behalf. When we become angry and emotional with our children it is typically because they are not being obedient in one way or another. When we encounter any scenario in which we have to deal with someone who is not listening to us, it can leave us feeling frustrated, to say the least, the same applies to our children but often on an even greater scale. We expect our children to listen to us and trust that we ask them to comply because we are their parents and have their best interests in mind. This is simply not a realistic expectation. Children naturally want to push the boundaries we set, and the way that we handle these challenges will typically determine the amount of defiance we will face as parents. We don't want our children to feel compelled to follow our instructions or meet the standards we set for them out of fear; this is one of the major issues that stem from angry parenting and creating negative associations for children. If we repeatedly act out in anger when our child does something we aren't happy about, we are essentially conditioning them. This is especially true if this response begins at a young age and our children are lead to believe that if they make a mistake, it makes them a bad person. This type of response can cause children to expect that we may not be there to provide them with a safe space to learn from those same mistakes. Having a child who behaves perfectly and wouldn't dare disobey a command because they are fearful of the repercussions in the sense that they may be verbally or physically attacked is not a situation any parent wants to find themselves in. There needs to be a high value placed on mutual respect between parent and child so that when issues do arise, they can communicate and solve these problems together.

Being a parent means that there will absolutely be times when we have to set rules and follow through with consequences for our children, but we can find ways to do these things while also being loving, caring, and nurturing. When our children trust us and feel confident in their abilities to meet realistic goals set forth through mutual agreement with their parents, they will be much more eager to work hard to succeed. Including children in the conversation regarding what is expected of them will help both sides understand where the other is coming from. If we do not provide our children with open channels of communication, they likely will not know how to do the same with their peers. Another consideration when addressing instances where we become angry with our child is the matter of how we want the experience to impact their internal monologue. Every time we talk to our child in a negative or angry way, we need to be conscientious of the fact that whether or not we mean the things we are saying while angry our child will hear them from the person who is supposed to love and care for them unconditionally. If a child hears their parents berating them and putting them down, then it is only natural for them to accept that some of what was said must be true. A child's sense of self-esteem and self-worth correlate directly to the messages they receive at home, so it is of the utmost importance to keep this in mind even when we get angry and raise our voice or express disappointment with our child. If we contribute to the development of a negative self-image and lack of confidence within our child, we are setting them up for a potential lifetime of abuse from peers and partners later on. It is generally accepted that many victims of bullying will be those who are struggling to accept themselves and find where they fit within the world around them.

As parents, we want to ensure we have a balance between the way we approach discipline and how we maintain an unwavering assurance of love and encouragement for our child. This relates to the idea that if we are raised in an environment that is always angry and reactive, we will most likely accept this in other areas of our lives. The thought of our child being bullied or abused by someone they trust and love is a nightmare for a parent. However, if we send our children out into the world believing that they have less worth because of mistakes they may have made, they are susceptible to becoming victims of those who prey on anyone with a perceived weakness to anger and control. Alternatively, we may also be setting our child up to become a perpetrator of angry and abusive behavior as they begin to develop new connections with the people they encounter in their own life. Our child could use the model we provided at home to become the bully by using fear tactics and aggression to control those around them. One of the even more concerning possibilities is if parents have set an example that when you are disappointed or angry with someone, the acceptable response is to get physical. By failing to manage our own anger, we may inadvertently teach our child that it is ok to hurt others.

It is inevitable that our children will have situations in which they become emotional and argue with a friend or partner. If their initial reaction is to become physical that could have much worse implications than just hurting someone with harsh words. Having the ability to solve problems, work through emotions, and develop a sense of empathy at home with their parents can help children take those same skills into the relationships they build outside of the family. We want our children to be as well-rounded and socially adept as possible; these skills are all things that we can teach and model at home so that they are picked up naturally.

The Reactions of Children to Parental Anger

Every parent hopes to have a strong and affable relationship with their children as they grow into adulthood. A common mistake is assuming that our children will maintain a relationship with us no matter how we treat them as children. After all, in our minds, we were simply acting as a parent and doing what we had to for their benefit. This is not the case, and increasingly adult children are distancing themselves from toxic parent relationships to ensure they can maintain their own mental and emotional health. The idea that we must tolerate people simply because they are family is becoming less and less commonplace. Today's world is full of what people refer to as "chosen family," and it consists of close friends who surround each other with love, trust, compassion, and a strong familial bond. If parents provide an upbringing full of anger, fear, resentment, and negative associations, they are running the risk of losing their bond with their children as soon as they are old enough to go out into the world on their own. This can be to varying degrees as some adult children will keep their parents at arm's length, which usually means they visit on holidays and try to keep in touch, but don't typically share much with their parents aside from general details that can be found on their public social media pages. Other adult children may completely cut ties with their parents as there are only ever negative interactions, memories of abuse, and continued toxicity and belittlement even as they have become independent. These are very real possibilities if a pattern of anger is repeated throughout their lives, and a trusting, loving relationship is never formed. It can be easy to dismiss the times when we act out of anger and justify them to ourselves as a necessary evil of parenthood, but at the end of the day, we may only be hurting ourselves by failing to manage our emotions for the betterment of our children's future.

Children begin to look up to their parents from the beginning of their lives. A parent is the first love and comfort a child will ever know, and if their relationship is treated with respect and a compassion then a parent will become a lifelong safe space for children even as they become adults and continue to face new challenges on their own. Although the impressions we have on our children will start from very early on, it is not impossible to repair any damage that may have been done as a result of our own shortcomings in terms of the management of our emotions and anger. In order to begin to change and rebuild trust and respect with our children, we must be willing to be honest and open with them. Accepting responsibility for our actions and the fact that we feel we have let them down is a major step to building a new foundation for the future. Being able to apologize to our children will provide them an opportunity to practice their ability to show empathy and is an example of the fact that everyone, even parents, is simply human and will make mistakes sometimes. Having an open and honest conversation with our children and developing a plan to move forward the same as we would if they were the ones who had done wrong will show that while there is a parent-child dynamic, you are still equals. This conversation is never easy, but ultimately it is worth the temporary discomfort to regain a healthy relationship with our children. This can be seen as a chance to start fresh and forgive each other for any struggles you have had to face together and a commitment to better communication as you move forward. There is no age limit for this to be feasible; however, it is much more likely to be effective if the relationship is still intact, even if only barely.

A child does not owe their parents unconditional love and forgiveness. As parents, we are always in a position to leverage our own emotional maturity and provide our children with the things they need to thrive, which are not just food, water, and a roof over their heads. Parents need to understand that we are responsible for treating our children with compassion, care, and in a way that earns their mutual respect as they grow and develop their own understanding of the world. To paraphrase a quote from Anne Lamott: "if you wanted your child to speak warmly of you, you should have behaved better." (Lamott, 1995).

THE IMPORTANCE OF SELF-CARE AS A PARENT

WHAT IS SELF CARE AND HOW CAN IT HELP ME?

Oftentimes as parents, we are so committed to tending to our children's needs that we neglect to meet our own. As mentioned multiple times already, parents are still people with emotions and are deserving of having their needs met. Taking some time to ensure our personal needs are also met will unarguably enable us to be much better parents. There are numerous ways that we can spend some time to care for ourselves, and ensuring we find the time to do so is just as important as making sure we show our children the love and care they need to thrive. It can be difficult for many people to take the first steps toward making themselves a priority. This is normal, but it is an obstacle we must overcome nonetheless to allow ourselves to become the caretakers our children deserve. Try to step back and look at the current conditions of your household. Whether there are two working parents or one who stays home full time with the kids, try to analyze how you, as parents, are interacting with the children. When there is no time for parents to indulge in some well-deserved self-care, this will leave you spread thin and forcing yourself to simply go through the motions of your daily routines.

While most parents juggle their responsibilities with being able to spend time with their children in a meaningful way, it can still rob families of the quality, fully engaged time together that they desire. When we fall into the rut of just trudging through every day until we get to bedtime, it can begin to feel like even the little things will set us off. Without taking the time to recharge our own mind and body, we can easily become overwhelmed with the seemingly never-ending list of chores, errands, and pressure we feel as parents. In terms of managing anger and emotional outbursts, there is not a much simpler change to make than finding a way to fit in some self-care once in a while. As with many things in life, it is easier said than done when it actually comes to making the change, but it is absolutely possible if we are willing to work on our ability to briefly disconnect from our parental role and do something that just makes us happy and relaxed in general.

Self-care is a broad term that encompasses anything you can think of that brings you joy and provides an opportunity to relax and recharge. The definition of self-care will vary from person to person, and there is really no right or wrong way to take some time for yourself. The main goal as a parent is to ensure the time, whether it is 20 minutes or 24 hours, is going to be spent focusing primarily on personal satisfaction. The first few times that we dedicate exclusively to taking care of our well-being, we will naturally struggle to let go of the worries, guilt, and the sense of selfishness that often comes with treating ourselves. Many of you have likely heard the term "mommy-guilt" (or daddy/parent guilt) used among parents, new and experienced alike. This is an extremely common sentiment, and it's something that I think every parent experiences at some point in their parenting journey and probably more than just the once. It is normal to feel a twinge of guilt about leaving our children in the care of someone besides ourselves for no reason other than to get some time away. People often mistakenly believe that by taking time away from our children, we are implying that we don't want to be around or don't enjoy the time we do spend with them. The opposite is actually true, and that is something we come to understand and accept as we begin to see the benefits of our self-care on our relationship with our children.

A strategy that can be used to help combat the guilty feelings we get, even though it is unwarranted, is to slowly work up to more time for ourselves. We don't have to jump into this type of change headfirst. It is entirely up to each parent how they would like to approach implementing some time for their needs. Start small and work your way up to whatever point you are comfortable with. This could mean starting with taking 10 minutes a day to sit alone on the porch with a coffee that is still hot (or at least warm...I did say start small), it could be taking 15 minutes to scroll social media, or even the simple act of having a shower without a child yelling at the bathroom door. The starting point is up to you, and it just has to be something that gives you a chance to breathe, clear your mind, and emerge feeling even only slightly less overwhelmed and worn down. The goal will be to progressively increase the amount of time dedicated to making yourself a priority. This will become easier as your children become more aware of the positive impact it has when their mommy, daddy, or caretaker is calm and energized. Without realizing, we can sometimes allow our built-up stress to influence how we interact with our children; in turn, this will contribute to the way they respond to us and the cycle will continue unless we step in to make a change. It is our duty as parents to recognize when there is a negative situation forming and ensure we make the necessary adjustments to avoid any damage to the relationship with our children. Everyone deserves the opportunity to have fun, relax, and enjoy their life. As a parent, we control the framework for our children's experience, and by making sure we are living a well-balanced life, we can provide the same opportunity for our children.

How can I practice Self-Care?

There are really infinite ways to practice self-care as a parent and just in general. These following suggestions are simply to provide some basic starting points and ideas. As you carve out more time for yourself and find a balance that suits your family's lifestyle you will find more ways to enjoy the time dedicated to doing something solely for your enjoyment. There are a few ways in which we can break down the different classifications of self-care and how we can approach giving ourselves fulfillment in the areas that benefit us most. Some people rely on having their physical needs met in order to be recharged and ready to tackle whatever their children, and life, can throw at them. Our physical needs are as unique as we are, and so is the way we go about making sure they are met. In some cases, we don't actually have to be alone when we practice self-care; we can include our family, friends, and even like-minded strangers in the activities we choose. Some options for getting physical to benefit our stress and emotional health are:

- The first and most obvious suggestion is to exercise in any way you enjoy and are comfortable. There are many options available to us to add more physical activity into our lives. Joining a gym and working either independently, with a trainer, or taking fitness classes can be the perfect way to help schedule some personal time into our busy lives. Having a set time for a class or training session can help arrange for childcare and prevent us from backing out of our plans at the last minute. Oftentimes these types of classes are also prepaid, which is a big motivation for many people to attend. Of course, there is no requirement to join a gym in order to move your body. Taking a leisurely walk can be just as effective at getting our exercise in and helping us feel good about our decision to make our health a priority too.
- Another great way to help keep our energy levels up and round out our physical health is by taking the time to eat well. The food we choose to put into

our bodies is the fuel we have to run on while running a household, working at home or elsewhere, and ultimately how we interact with our children. It can be difficult to prepare healthy balanced meals when we are juggling so many other tasks, and if taking some time to get organized and prepare ahead can help with meeting a goal of healthier eating, then it is a great way to implement some self-care.

- There is a common saying that when we look good, we will also start to feel good. There is nothing wrong with using your personal time to go get pampered and give yourself a confidence boost in the meantime. Men and women both deserve to feel their best, and if that means getting their hair or nails done, then that is exactly what they should do. A change in our style or just refreshing a go-to look can work wonders for our physical and emotional health. If that isn't something that interests you, maybe consider a facial or a massage to help eliminate some of the tension and stress that we hold in our muscles. There is no doubt that when we get older, things start to ache a little more, and it can certainly impact our mood at times.
- Something that can often be put on the back burner

when we become parents is making sure we are spending some time with our partners outside of our parental roles. This can be in the form of taking some time to share how we are feeling to share some emotional intimacy, or it can be time spent together being physically intimate. The focus on raising children, working long hours, maintaining a household, and trying to fit a good night's sleep in there too, can take a toll on our ability to spend the quality time we desire with our partners. Maintaining a strong connection requires contributions from both sides in a relationship and can be a way to destress that many overlook.

The next section is one that many people feel they are lacking in fulfillment because it can be difficult to overcome the parenting guilt that comes along with actually getting out and away from your children. As difficult as it may be, this is another important area to consider when selecting ways to add self-care to your routine. Humans are social by nature, and we crave connections with others to some extent. Taking care of our social and emotional wellness can help us when we return to our children and family and put our parenting hat back on. There are plenty of ways to meet these needs, and some suggestions to get started are:

- Just getting out to spend some time out of the home, even if it means having your children with you. Making sure you are not sitting inside staring at the same four walls day in and day out can have a positive impact on our mental health and ability to better regulate emotions. Whether this means you leave your children in the care of someone you trust and head out on your own to a favorite location, or it could be taking your children along with you to a park or beach. Whatever will work best for you and allow you to enjoy a change of scenery and maybe some fresh air. Bring your children to a playground and take a break on the bench while they run around a few feet away. This is a safe way to let them meet their own physical needs while you take care of your emotional ones. Bonus points if you meet a friend or family member on that park bench and get a chance to socialize with someone who doesn't call you mom or dad.
- Social interactions are important and should be prioritized as much as possible. Scheduling a date night with your partner or night out with friends can be a great way to get out of the house and keep yourself occupied to avoid some of that parental guilt. There is really no right way to plan an adult-

only date; it can be any time of day that fits into your schedule. A meal, a group event like a room escape or paint night, or a cup of coffee with friends, there are no rules to follow. Finding the time to reconnect with old friends and have fun without worrying about our children is a healthy way to take a break while managing our emotional needs.

Finally, there are some ways that we can utilize our personal downtime to help meet our spiritual needs. This is a major part of many people's lives, and while it can absolutely be related to religious devotion, the definition of spiritual can apply to anything that benefits our mind and soul.

- We can foster a sense of spiritual enrichment by serving others. Scheduling some time to do any actions that benefit others can be a great way to help us center ourselves and feel good about what we accomplished in doing so. This could be achieved by doing some volunteer work with any cause you support, tidying up litter in your neighborhood park or natural space, or even just by spending time helping someone with a task.
- People who hold religious beliefs can also find joy and comfort in attending religious services, prayer groups, or even doing some introspective reflection on how they serve themselves and others around them.
- If you don't have any specific religious beliefs, you can always meditate and focus on releasing stress and tension while clearing your mind. There are plenty of in-depth resources available for meditation, as well as guided meditation videos or audio recordings.

The important thing is to take the steps necessary to become comfortable with occasionally putting yourself first. It is a sign of a good parent to be able to prioritize their mental health and actively improve their ability to regulate their emotions. Never feel ashamed or guilty for making every effort to provide your children with the best possible environment and modeling a healthy, well-rounded lifestyle.

PARENTING STYLES TO CONSIDER

WHAT ARE PARENTING STYLES

Many people will naturally take an approach that is similar to the way their parents raised them. There is not often the consideration of whether or not the methods of their parents included traditional discipline or if they normalized angry behavior within the home. It is not for me to say whether any one family's parenting style may be right or wrong. Still, there are some techniques that can be incorporated into whichever parenting approach we decide to take. They have the potential to provide a more positive and gentle environment for parents and children alike. The aim of this entire eBook is to help guide parents through some of the ways they can better manage their anger and provide a more calm and patient response to their children as they grow.

There is no claim that there is a one-size-fits-all solution to help every parent become infallible and raise their children to be the same. If anyone were to try and factually present that there was one correct way to go about being more patient with our children, I would have a difficult time believing that there was truly any evidence supporting that statement. There are, in fact, many different ways that people choose to go about parenting, and the classifications have been changing and evolving in recent years as there is more information to support the different effects certain methods may have on children. The commonly discussed styles, some of which you have likely heard of, are:

Authoritarian Parenting

This is focused primarily on the principle that children are to be obedient at all times and will be punished if they fail to meet the expectations of these types of parents. There is more prevalence of physical punitive measures in this style and often a lack of emotional compassion between parent and child. Children who are raised by parents with an authoritarian approach are prone to mirror this behavior in their own lives and in the future if they become parents themselves. There can be some troubling ramifications of choosing this parenting style without making a few changes to adapt to common societal norms surrounding the discipline and emotional well-being of children.

Neglectful or Uninvolved Parenting

This style is often considered to be lazy parenting and is especially abhorred by parents who follow more strict authoritarian views. The neglectful or uninvolved parent is one who will allow their child to do whatever keeps them entertained and doesn't create any issues for the parents that require tending to. This often leads to an excess of screen time and a lack of meaningful time spent together as a family unit. There can be a long-term impact on children raised by parents who were not very involved in their upbringings, such as under-development of communication skills, less motivation to succeed than children of other styled parents, and various mental and emotional issues due to a lack of parental nurturing. This is only a generalization and may not be the outcome for all children who are raised in homes with very little parental involvement, but it is widely accepted that this is not the best balance in terms of parental control and children's development of independence. This style of parenting can stem from issues on the parent's end, such as untreated mental health issues, addictions, alcoholism, and many other socioeconomic factors. As a result of these often preexisting conditions, some children may experience parentification and be forced to take care of themselves, siblings, and even parents during their own formative years.

Permissive or Indulgent Parenting

This style is characterized by parents who are full of love, nurturing, and compassion for their children; however, they fail to apply any real structure or firm expectations. There will often be difficulties for both the child and their parent when it comes to determining where the line between friend and parent is drawn. As well-intentioned as these parents may be, there is still a risk of their children failing to learn what is right and wrong in society because they were very rarely told no. The rules are often extremely flexible and allow children to dictate what is acceptable for them to do, where they can go, with who, and when they will do it. This type of freedom given to children can have a positive impact on their ability to express themselves, identify their desires, and willingness to explore the world around them. On the same note, they may also expect to be catered to and have a hard time when they are eventually told no by someone they cannot manipulate or supersede. Because of the relaxed environment and minimal parental control, these children may also be at risk for parentification and consider themselves more mature than they are developmentally capable of being.

Authoritative Parenting

This is often referred to as being the ideal approach to parenting, and I tend to agree, but as mentioned at the beginning of this chapter, it is important to remember that there is no perfect solution that will fit every family every time. This type of parenting incorporates different areas of the styles mentioned above and creates the best balance between providing structure and rules while also allowing children to become independent and make mistakes. There is often a sliding scale for the amount of freedom children receive, and it is dependent on their proven ability to make good choices, building a trusting relationship with their parents, and openly communicating when issues arise. There are still elements of an authoritarian parenting style in the sense that these parents believe in consequences for the actions of children, but there is not a high instance of physical punishment or a "because I said so" approach. Communication and understanding are key in this parenting style, and helping children learn from their mistakes while accepting the consequences of them is a large part of this emotionally in-touch approach. Children who have parents following a variation of this style will typically be emotionally intelligent themselves, have an easier time forming and maintaining relationships throughout their lives, and being able to navigate social situations both professionally and personally. Parents are also increasingly moving to incorporate aspects of what is known as "empathic parenting" into this style as well. There is a heavy focus on instilling empathy in their children and taking care to demonstrate empathy toward them as well. This specific style of parenting is beneficial as it helps both parents and children understand the emotions of the other and how they may be impacted as a result.

Another common trend with authoritative parents is embracing the concept of intuitive or attachment parenting. This very literally means allowing parental intuition to guide them through the process of raising their child. This is a very natural approach to child-rearing and usually results in a very strong attachment bond between parents and children from a young age. There are components of permissive, authoritarian, and the more niche empathic parenting, all intertwined within the attachment parenting style. If it is a viable option for your family and lifestyle, the resulting ease of the ever-deepening relationship with your child can result in much more open channels of communication and, in turn, fewer triggers for anger.

These different styles are the breakdown of some of the general ways parents raise their children. This information is helpful to guide us in making decisions for our children and when analyzing how we may have been affected by the way we were raised by our own parents. There are other techniques that can be applied in combination with these methods to enhance our anger management and to aid in creating a more calm and patient parenting experience for ourselves as well as providing our children with the most enriching childhood possible.

When Parents Have Differing Opinions on Parenting Style

There may be times when parents, biological, step-parents, or otherwise, may have differing opinions regarding how to approach parenting. This can present some issues because it is important that children see their parents as a united front. There cannot be visible weak points, or children will often learn how to take advantage of these issues and create more strife amidst an existing struggle. Parents may face some significant hurdles when they find they don't agree on parenting styles; handling this amongst themselves is imperative to providing a safe and healthy parenting experience for their child. If it is an option to sit down and discuss their ideal approach to parenting, they may be able to avoid many issues in the future. In a situation where these concerns only surface later on, as their children are growing or a family dynamic changes, then educating themselves and each other on their respective beliefs is recommended, so both parties understand what the other is seeking from their partner. Supporting each other and not allowing the child to exploit the differing opinions is also an important factor in managing the ability to care for your child. Finding common ground between both parents' desired parenting method can be a good starting point. This might mean analyzing the specific beliefs and expectations each parent has for the children and determining where there are similarities or even overlapping characteristics that both parents can agree to support moving forward. There will need to be some flexibility on the part of both parents and a willingness to communicate what they feel is working and what could be done differently.

Parenting styles can evolve and will often need to adapt to changing situations within the home and from outside influences. Setting out a specific set of guidelines that both parents can agree to will help enforce them with their children and also help children understand exactly what is expected of them in terms of behavior and the development of their role within the family. If there seems to be no resolution and they are unable to reach an agreement, then parents might benefit from seeking outside help in the form of parenting classes or even family counseling for everyone involved, provided the children are old enough to participate as well.

8

FINDING CALM THROUGH THE FIRST YEAR STORM

DEVELOPMENT AND TRIGGERS IN THE FIRST YEAR

The first year of parenthood is full of some of the most amazing moments many of us will have experienced up to that point in our lives. While the advice is well-intentioned, people always seem to tell new parents to enjoy every minute of it, sleep when your baby sleeps, and that things get easier as our babies grow out of the newborn phase. For some parents, this may be helpful and ring true, but for others, this may make them feel worse when they struggle to enjoy every minute. While we are receiving this advice, we are focused mainly on trying to balance the addition of an entirely dependent new little human to our family and making sure we eat, sleep, and bathe. The physical and mental toll that the first few weeks, or months in some cases, with a new baby, will take on us as parents can leave us exhausted and emotionally raw. It is not news to anyone that when we feel overwhelmed, tired, hungry, and every other emotion imaginable, the chances of us losing our cool over something small are much higher than before we began this new chapter of our lives.

Becoming a parent is supposed to be a joyous moment in our lives, so why do we find ourselves feeling so many overwhelmingly negative emotions all the time? The answer to that question is that there are many contributing factors, and if we are more aware of why we are feeling the way we are, we can take some steps to make the adjustment easier on everyone. Both parents will be experiencing physical changes after bringing home a new baby. Mothers and fathers alike will have hormonal changes in response to their child, their new roles as protectors, and the lack of sleep. There are tons of changes that take place during this time, and they are generally out of our control, so it is important that we do our best to minimize the impact of, and manage, the other factors when we are able to. The first thing to remember as a new parent is that no two babies will be the exact same. Babies have their own temperaments and preferences in regard to how their needs are met by parents and caregivers. It can be especially difficult to hear a friend or family member tell you how easy their baby was as a newborn when you are already knee-deep in anxiety, stress, the fear of failure, and dirty diapers. Taking the advice and anecdotes of others with a few grains of salt is definitely recommended. There is no benefit to comparing your child to someone else's at this stage because all babies respond to the transition from womb to room differently, and it can be difficult to accept that concept once we have formed arbitrary expectations based on the experiences of others. It is okay to ask for advice and guidance but don't write your own handbook based on someone else's story. At the end of the day, the characters are different, and what works for one parent may be the total opposite for another.

Accepting that our baby is unique will help us learn how to respond to their needs, take care of our own, and adapt with them as we grow together. One of the major triggers for new parents is the amount of crying their baby will do in the first few months after they are born. Everyone expects that babies will cry, of course; however, the reality of how often and how loud our baby can scream is sometimes shocking. Babies are not born with any sort of understanding of how to communicate or express their own emotions, so they react the way it is most natural and effective for humans to alert others that they are in need. Whether a baby needs something physical like a diaper change or to be fed or if they are feeling emotional distress of some sort, they are only going to use their instinctual reaction, which is to cry out for their parent's attention.

It is absolutely an overwhelming experience while we are trying to decipher what the cause of their upset may be, and in the beginning, it may actually end up being nothing in particular, which is known as "purple crying." This term is sometimes used synonymously with "colic" and can be a very difficult time for parents with babies who experience it. Purple crying is characterized by extended periods of crying despite there being no identifiable cause and no presence of any medical concerns after the baby is seen by a doctor. This phase can last anywhere from a few weeks to a couple of months and can present new parents with some unexpected challenges to their already fragile emotional health. The term use of the word 'purple' to describe this phase is actually an acronym which stands for:

- **Peak of Crying:** The phase can start around 2 weeks, peaking around 2 months, and typically becoming less severe through months 3 to 5
- **Unexpected:** Crying may come and go throughout this phase with no apparent cause
- **Resists Soothing:** No matter what tired and

concerned parents try, their efforts to soothe their baby are ineffective
- **Pain-Like Face:** Babies may appear to be in pain even though they are not
- **Long-Lasting:** The crying may go on for 5 hours or more per day
- **Evening:** The bouts of crying are more often later in the day and into the evening

While this experience is very troubling for parents who experience it, it is also noted that this is referred to as a phase or period of purple crying, which means it will come to an end. Being aware that this is a possibility when bringing home a new baby can help prepare for it and have a plan in place in case you do end up feeling angry, frustrated, and emotionally overwhelmed. When we do everything in our power to meet our baby's needs, and it still doesn't seem to be working, it can cause us to feel like we are failing when in reality, it is a normal behavior for young infants to go through. In a situation like this, we need to accept that we have exhausted our options, and it is in the best interest of our baby and ourselves to take a few moments to recharge and allow our minds to clear and take a break from the crying. If we allow ourselves to remain in the presence of our crying baby after we find ourselves becoming angry and helpless, it is possible that some people may react angrily toward their infant. This type of response is rarely intentional, and parents don't expect that it is something they are capable of, to begin with, but there are cases of people screaming at, shaking, and even hitting their babies to try and stop their crying. This is a purely emotional impulse that can be avoided by taking some steps to ensure our baby is safe, and we can get the break we need. If this type of scenario is unfolding in your home, please ask for help from a partner, friend, or family member if possible. Have someone take over for just a few minutes to allow you to take the time you need to calm down and take a step back. In a situation when there is no one around to relieve you, simply put your baby down in a safe place (think: crib, bassinet, playpen) and walk away from the crying for a moment.

It is much more conducive to calm and patient parenting to take a minute when you know you need it than to try and force yourself or your infant to adjust immediately. Keeping in mind that babies cry and it is the only way they can communicate with their parents is helpful when it feels like crying is all they do. Infants spend a lot of time sleeping and crying in the first few months, and then once the crying becomes less frequent, their time spent awake will increase as they develop and begin to interact with their surroundings for the first time. Each new stage that our babies reach will bring about new challenges for both the parents and baby, so we want to make an effort to develop a trusting bond early on so we can tackle the obstacles together.

Taking a Calm and Patient Approach Early On

Knowing that babies are all different but that all babies communicate by crying will help in figuring out how best to approach the emotions that affect us as parents. One thing that many parents swear by, even as their children grow older, is implementing a routine in some way. Having a routine can help provide children with structure and a guideline to follow throughout the day, and this can help them understand and manage expectations from an early age. Babies are heavily influenced by their physical needs and can become much more difficult to manage if they are hungry, uncomfortable in terms of being too warm or too cold, have a wet diaper, become tired, or even if they are experiencing sensory overload. These are some of the core basics to watch out for to try and head off some of the more frustrating behaviors we endure with babies. If our baby is signaling to us that they are tired and we miss those cues, then we can allow them to become overtired. Many parents may believe that an overtired baby will fall asleep easier at that point, and in some cases, that may be true, but more often than not, an overtired infant will become very fussy and difficult to soothe.Developing a routine that follows our baby's cues in terms of when to eat and sleep can be a great technique for avoiding meltdowns for both baby and parent. It will take a little bit of time to figure out what works for your child, but if you practice intuitive parenting and pay attention to how your baby's behavior changes when they are signaling it is time to eat or sleep, then you can start to solidify the steps of your routine and perfect it over time.

Sometimes we may need to take some extra steps outside of the routine if our baby reaches the point of being overtired or when they are experiencing a period of purple crying. Many parents find it works to strap their baby safely into their car seat and go for a drive. You can play gentle lullabies or some white noise to help relax yourself and your baby; it is a safe place for us to take a break and provide our baby with a change of scenery. Taking the opportunity early on to begin a gentle approach to parenting and responding to your child's needs can also be helpful when it comes to avoiding parental anger and emotional discomfort of your baby. The more time a parent dedicates to building a strong bond and intuitive response to their child, the easier it will be to gauge when the child feels emotionally vulnerable and in need of comfort from mom or dad. Physical connection is very important for babies as it helps them develop a sense of being loved and cared for and lets them know that they are safe within their parent's embrace. Take some time to snuggle up with your baby for some quiet moments together outside of soothing them when they express that they are upset. Slowing down and allowing ourselves to enjoy being our baby's first lesson in love and comfort can be one of the most simple yet rewarding experiences we have in the first year.

PATIENCE FOR THE TODDLER AND PRESCHOOL YEARS

DEVELOPMENT OF TODDLERS AND PRESCHOOLERS

It is not uncommon to hear people describe their toddler as being in their "terrible twos" or saying they woke up with a "threenager." These sayings have become popular because they tend to be quite apt at describing the behavior of our young children as they begin to develop emotionally and intellectually at a much quicker pace than they had been in the first year. The first few years of our children's lives are undoubtedly full of exciting new opportunities to play, laugh, and begin to share our own interests with them. Make sure to remind yourself that there are so many rewarding milestones and memories made during these years of exploration and learning. It is ok to struggle as the parent of an energetic toddler. I don't think any parent out there can say they sailed through this period with ease. Children are all different, and the characteristics that form their personalities are going to vary; this is where parents of multiple children can be thrown off with a second (or any additional) child who may be the polar opposite of their sibling. A common tip in this eBook is to remain flexible and be willing to adapt to the needs and challenges of each unique child. As our children enter into toddlerhood, our previously developed routine can be altered to fit their schedule as they continue to grow and their needs change. Maintaining a routine with our toddler will provide some consistency in terms of the expectations we have for them and eventually guide them to being more intuitive themselves. As parents, we want to help our children identify their needs and how to address them appropriately. Doing our best to establish a routine that works for both our children and us can be the framework for the boundaries and non-negotiable expectations we will set forth as they get older.

Keeping a toddler busy and stimulated can be a good way to manage their energy and curiosity that can sometimes lead to frustrating behavior for parents. Try to have a variety of age-appropriate toys on hand for children in this age group and, if possible, rotate them every so often so they can spend some time exploring something different. It may be tempting to fall into some uninvolved parenting style approaches at this age because there is an endless stream of cartoons and videos available that are specifically targeting children under the age of five. There is no harm in allowing children to enjoy a cartoon or movie within reason, but it is recommended that they also take part in some activities that will help them develop motor skills as well as their intellectual skills. Some hands-on toys that can be good for toddlers are things like puzzles with large pieces, sensory toys, supervised use of coloring and craft materials, and soft toys. There are also all kinds of educational toys available that can help appease the curiosity of toddlers with buttons, lights, and music that can also have educational components.

There is no guaranteed method to avoid the occasional meltdowns and tantrums, however, we can use these behaviors to practice empathy and offer a chance for our child to understand what is acceptable in terms of managing their feelings. When our toddlers or preschoolers assert their independence or throw a tantrum, we have to ensure we are doing our best to model how to respond to negative emotions. We will be angry at times and likely catch ourselves raising our voice in response to our 3-year-old saying "no" for the hundredth time that afternoon, that is a normal reaction, and it doesn't mean we are failing. When this happens, try to be mindful of the fact that our child is only now learning that they can be independent and it is very exciting and emboldening for them. Set the tone for the conversation by choosing to talk calmly and gently, be consistent and firm when there is a need to discipline your little one. Remember that if we use our size or strength to yell and hit our toddlers, they will not comprehend the reason behind it and will often become more defiant while mirroring our negative behavior.

As children progress through their toddler and preschool years, it will become more common for them to have the really big emotions that got them the nickname "terrible two" and "threenager." Temper tantrums can begin anytime around the age of one and continue until they learn how to better manage the emotions behind them. Much like parents who are reading this eBook to better manage their own anger to stay calm, toddlers are still learning about the feelings they experience and how to work through them. There is very little understanding about the feelings of others at this age, especially when they are struggling emotionally themselves. Trying to reason with an upset toddler can be nearly impossible, but it can be helpful to try and get down on their level while using a gentle tone and offer them some kind words. The fact that we understand how it feels to be overwhelmed can help some parents put their own frustration aside to help their child try to work through the moment and worry about addressing the negative behavior after they have calmed down.

As children get closer to the age of four and five, they are going to be more capable of identifying and discussing their emotions, and with the help of their parents, they may also be able to explore what made them feel that way. Children can also begin to develop fears around the age of three and upward, which can lead to some emotional outbursts that may cause parents to lose their patience. Be mindful that the fears of toddlers and preschoolers are very real in their minds, and to dismiss them will usually only cause them to become even more emotionally distressed. Take the time to acknowledge what they are feeling and help them to work through this just as you would if they were angry over a broken toy or being told they couldn't have ice cream for dinner. The experience they are having is scary to them, whether or not we can understand why they believe there is a three-eyed monster in their closet. Helping our children learn to navigate their emotions will help instill a sense of emotional intelligence early on and give them a good foundation to build on as they develop emotionally.

Including children of this age in decisions, when possible, can also help them connect with how they are feeling and provide an opportunity to exert their independence without causing them to act out and break the rules we have set for them. Depending on the child's maturity level and age, we can start by offering a couple of options to choose from. As they progress up to school age, they can be asked to provide options for their parents or give an open-ended response when asked to make a choice.

The last couple of years in this age group can be very challenging for parents because their child is now capable of communicating a lot more but hasn't fully developed their understanding of how their actions impact those around them. This can cause some issues in terms of children wanting to share, becoming aggressive when they don't get their way, and suffering from mood swings when they are dealing with a lot of emotional turbulence. The use of time out as a consequence for negative behaviors can prove effective for some children, and it can be easily explained that this is an opportunity for them to reflect on their behavior and to think of any questions they may have for their parents. This type of punishment should be age-appropriate and used as a stepping stone to reaching a positive resolution. We can also use this time to breathe and mentally reset after dealing with a frustrating child. Coming back from a few moments of time out for both parent and child can allow the cooldown time necessary to be able to have a productive conversation about how to handle similar situations going forward. This won't work every time, but it is a good technique to try when both people are in need of some time, and the parent is able to regain control of their own emotions to better guide the child through theirs.

As children approach the end of this age group, they tend to become much less combative and defiant, and they are more willing to follow the rules, especially when parents explain why they set the boundaries that they do and how it will impact everyone if these rules are broken. Making every effort to provide our children with the skills they will need to move forward into their school-aged years is imperative to their success as they move on to one of the biggest changes they will experience thus far. If it is an option to have our children interact with others through playgroups or organized activities, it can help them learn about sharing and playing with other children in a more relaxed setting with a trusted parent present. It can be one of the more frustrating and draining periods for some parents and even more so if they have multiple children in the home and need to divide their attention between them.

There are going to be times when your toddler will cause you to lose your cool and throw attempts at patience out the window. We have the ability to decide what happens next and whether or not we will control the situation or allow our emotions to control us. When a slip-up does happen, just apologize to your child and explain that it's the same as if they were to make a mistake or get angry and hit or scream. Our children look up to us for guidance on how to conduct themselves, even if that means saying sorry when we mess up. Teaching our toddlers that we are all human is a lesson in empathy and compassion that they will be able to carry with them into adulthood. The reward for remaining patient and being a gentle parent comes when we get to enjoy the moments of calm we spend with our children. There is no better feeling than when your child crawls into your lap, snuggles into your arms, and rests their head on your shoulder. Cherish these moments; they are just what we need on those days that we are sure we have failed as parents.

10

MANAGING ANGER WITH SCHOOL AGED KIDS

DEVELOPMENT OF SCHOOL AGED CHILDREN

Once our children enter their grade school years, they become fully exposed to other children and authority figures that are not their parents. With this new environment comes the influence of everything outside of the considerably smaller bubble they have been living in up to this point. The age range for this developmental stage is quite broad and encompasses ages five or six right up to the age of twelve. The development of a child will be drastically different by the end of this stage than it was when they began. Understanding the changes that school-aged children go through can help parents better relate to them while enabling them to learn some healthy coping mechanisms for when they are angry or emotional themselves. If parents continue to demonstrate positive ways to channel their energy and emotions, their children will be more likely to have an easier transition to becoming even more independent teenagers.

One thing that children tend to do in these first years of independent exploration is to test the previously established boundaries that parents have enforced. This behavior is normal and helps children learn how to exert self-control in terms of following rules and respecting those who are enforcing them. However, no matter how many times we are reminded that certain behaviors are, in fact, developmentally normal, it does not change the fact that they are still very challenging for parents. We can get into a comfortable place with our toddler and preschool children who seem to have finally learned how to follow rules, respect others, and to use their indoor voices even when they get mad. As we venture into this new stage it can be very discouraging when we start to notice our child is constantly stepping over the lines of the boundaries we worked so hard to impose. Our children will now be developing a better understanding of emotions themselves and are able to use them to manipulate their parents into reacting negatively or becoming exhausted and giving in to their child's bad behavior. Make every effort to stay consistent and firm in terms of the response to these instances when your child decides to test the limits of your patience. It is their goal to see just how far they can get before they anger or ideally breakdown the parent's will to enforce the rules of which the child does not wish to adhere. If the child receives an indication that they have succeeded in pushing their parent even slightly over the threshold of acceptable behavior, they will often take advantage of this and continue their attempts to cross the line while avoiding punishment. Explaining why there are certain rules and guidelines in place can help children cooperate in following them, and the more honest communication between parent and child, the better. As with the previous developmental stages, our children will be starting to experience new stronger emotions that can cause them to react angrily with an outburst or a harder to read temper tantrum. There will be times that it may not be immediately obvious why our young children are acting out, but if we can continue the process of discussing emotions together, it will be much easier to dissect the situation and help address the root of the negative behavior.

Early on in this stage, children will often begin to develop a concept of jealousy, whether it is in the form of wanting something another child has or not getting the attention they see siblings or others receiving from a loved one. As adults, we know that feeling envious of someone else can make us quite angry and occasionally causes some people to act irrationally. There are times when a much more emotionally developed adult will act passive-aggressive out of jealousy, and in some cases, people will even be openly aggressive to try and quell the anger associated with the desire to have something someone else has. Our young children are just as susceptible to experiencing jealousy but are much less equipped to manage the negative emotions that come along with it. If your child is angry or hurt by the fact that they feel they have not been given the same amount of attention as a sibling or other child, then it is important to address those feelings and explain that no matter what the circumstances, they are loved by and important to their parents. Getting angry as a response to a child expressing their struggle with jealousy will only cause them to internalize these feelings in the future and lead to tantrums, negative associations, and a breakdown of trust and communication. Instead of forcing our children to accept that they must share their toys or the attention of their loved ones without question, we should strive to explain to them that even when they may feel like someone else has something they don't, it is ok to be upset, but that at the same time everyone has needs that need to be met physically and emotionally. Teach your child to share their toys so that they are able to experience positive emotions when they see a friend or sibling enjoying the toy and explain that even though mommy and daddy spend time with other siblings or family members, they will always make time for the child as well. Learning that there will be times when they cannot obtain immediate gratification can help develop their understanding of patience, compassion for others, and a sense of self-control. Building these skills and developing the ability to apply them to their own actions will be very useful as children enter school, and they will be placing a much higher importance on the relationships they are forming outside of their family unit.

Throughout the first few years of school, most children will create strong bonds with classmates, teammates, and any other children they meet beyond this. These friendships will be extremely important to our children. They will use the behavior their parents modeled as they navigate the waters of being a good friend, conflict resolution, and respecting others' personal boundaries. As you notice your child is developing shared interests with their friends and becoming closer with different social groups, it is a good opportunity to discuss peer pressure. The conversation will evolve as your children continue to grow and meet new people with different levels of influence on their decision making and how they define what cool or acceptable behavior is. There may be times when your child comes home and has picked up on some undesirable new habits, words, opinions, etc. that were shared by a friend at school. Most children don't have a very effective filter when it comes to telling their friends about things their own parents have said or done, so it is important to address any issues with things your child has learned elsewhere without talking poorly about their friend or their parents. Depending on the severity of the issue, there may be a valid reason to reach out to the other parents and discuss how best to address it, but it is always best to do this privately and not to use it as a threat to elicit change or new information from your child. Encourage your child to think things through on their own and determine if they feel something is a positive or negative behavior. Allowing our children to explore the things they learn from others, whether we agree with them or not, can help them develop leadership skills and a moral compass to guide them through the inevitable peer pressures to come into their teenage years. If we allow our children to have some of the independence they crave at this age, they will be much better prepared to handle more difficult situations as they get older and have less supervision.

Make an effort to find some balance between your child's independence and being able to take the reins when they require a little bit more structure to keep them safe and on track. It may feel like the easiest way to handle our own emotions is to try and instill fear through punishment when our child says or does something wrong. However, it will only teach them that if they get caught, they will have consequences as a result. Learning at a young age to hide negative behavior and try to cover up mistakes will not benefit anyone as our children become teenagers and young adults. Since children in this age group are typically able to understand the reason we have rules in place, we can also allow them to provide input regarding their expectations. Allowing them to express what they want and what they feel is fair can be a good tool for finding punishments that both sides feel are appropriate for the behavior or the rule that was broken. Taking an approach of positive reinforcement can be effective with children in this age group, which is why many teachers will use sticker chart systems that reward good behavior and either punish bad behavior or don't acknowledge it at all. The emotions that come with being recognized for completing tasks, meeting goals, and displaying positive behaviors can be very constructive when it comes to forming habits and avoiding the negative associations with traditional punishment.

Helping our children understand that their actions have an effect on those around them, and accepting that the same is true for the actions of others can prove to be a very simple yet pragmatic approach. Young children want to feel like they are a part of everything and ultimately strive to copy their parents and those they are closest to. Using positive reinforcement and building their confidence to make good decisions can set them up for a smoother transition into the emotional rollercoaster that comes with puberty and the teenage years.

PATIENT PARENTING WITH TEENAGERS

TAKING ON THE TEENAGE YEARS

It is common to have people wish you luck as you enter the teenage years with your child, and as a result, it can be downright intimidating when that thirteenth birthday rolls around. The behavior of teenagers can be a challenge for most parents; if we are also dealing with trying to manage our own anger, it can become exponentially more difficult for everyone. Learning how to engage with your teenage child in a productive and positive way is an extremely important skill. By the time our children reach their teen years, they will be starting to process thoughts and emotions differently, things become less clear cut, and teens may struggle to understand why things are the way they are. It is more important than ever to avoid taking a stance of "that's just how it is." or "because I said so, that's why!" when your teenager challenges the rules and expectations. By this point in our parenting journey, it has become clear that being consistent and assertive in our approach to discipline is a major factor when it comes to striking a balance between our child's independence and our responsibilities as their parents. Being consistent does not mean that we have to be unmoving; however, being flexible and willing to adapt and compromise on some things may help show that we have faith in our teen's ability to make good choices. If we can find ways to include our teenagers in the decision-making process regarding the expectations and boundaries we have for them, they will be much more likely to follow them willingly.

This exciting time in our child's life can be especially unnerving for us as parents as we realize how soon they will be moving on into adulthood and taking on the responsibility of caring for themselves with the whole world at their fingertips. We must keep in mind that imposing too many rules or unreasonable expectations will usually cause teens to either rebel and push back against us or to develop lower self-esteem due to the belief that they are perpetually failing to meet their parent's standards. Every child is going to develop at their own pace. There is no set age that denotes a teenager is ready to be given more trust and responsibility, but we must provide them with opportunities to prove their abilities to make the right choices and learn from their mistakes. Keeping your child involved in the decisions regarding what rules they must follow as well as the consequences if they fail to do so will create an environment of mutual respect and reduce the child's desire to purposely test the threshold for your tolerance of negative behavior. When there are times that punishment or consequence is necessary, it is not a good idea to impulsively throw out empty threats to your teen. This is a pattern a teenager will pick up on very quickly and exploit to their benefit as they see fit. For example, if your child knows the expectation is that they have their room clean each Sunday before bed, but you had threatened to throw away their belongings for the past three weeks when it wasn't done, they are going to continue to push the limit to see how far they can go before you reach your patience threshold. Considering that most of our children's things will be items that we have purchased for them, it is not reasonable to tell our child we will throw it all away if they don't keep it tidy. Sticking to predetermined consequences is going to be much more effective and conducive to a positive resolution. If we adhere to the guidelines we have set with our child, then there is very little room for argument when the time comes to implement the punishment. We have to ensure that when we decide on a set of rules and the applicable consequences that we are sticking to those guidelines and enforcing them consistently. If we decided that our child would lose their cell phone for one day per thirty-minute period they are past curfew, it would be unreasonable to then take their phone for a week if they arrived home forty minutes late. Being flexible and finding middle ground on which both parent and child can agree will help teach our children about the importance of following through on the commitments we make while also showing compassion and a willingness to compromise on what both sides consider to be a fair punishment.

Ways to Mitigate Conflict With Teenagers

Our teenage children face some major changes throughout the years leading up to adulthood, and it can be confusing and often scary to navigate the emotions and pressure that come with those changes. Puberty is well-known for being one of the most difficult transitions people experience at any point in life. The emotions and hormones that arise throughout the beginning stages of adolescence are extreme and can be embarrassing for many teenagers. Be sure to take the time to openly discuss the changes with your child and provide them with educational material that they can review on their own when they feel a little bit more comfortable. It doesn't have to be an awkward conversation if we have allowed our children to express their curiosity freely, answered questions about their body truthfully, and reinforced the fact that we are there to help them with anything they need as they grow. Avoiding the fact that our children are going through major physical and mental changes can just leave them feeling confused, frightened, and following the guidance and influence of their friends, which is often a recipe for disaster when it comes to pubescent teens.

There is a lot of pressure on teens when it comes to being accepted and fitting in with their friends. Sometimes, that means they change their behavior to mirror the friends and peers they are seeking approval from. With the accessibility of information on the internet now, things are much different than they were for children even just a decade ago. Making sure that our children are receiving accurate information and forming realistic expectations of themselves and their peers can help them manage their emotions and reduce some of the uncertainty around their developing bodies and minds. As a teenager, the desire to engage in emotionally and physically romantic relationships will begin, and it often hits hard and unexpectedly. When we discuss the changes that come along with being a teenager it is important to address this as well to avoid having our children engaging in risky behaviors with consequences they were not mature enough to foresee. Many teens will enter into relationships that they consider to be mature and serious commitments. While it is not fair to diminish the emotions that are involved in these relationships, it is absolutely our job as parents to help our child manage the expectations of their partner and understand the potential consequences of their actions. Talking to your child about sex can help avoid confusion and anger that results from misjudging a situation and the ensuing embarrassment. We cannot respond to our child's natural, while still developing and misguided, impulse to explore their sexuality and changing bodies.

Showing our children empathy and compassion will help them understand that as complicated as this period may be, it is normal, and they are still loved and cared for by their parents. In some cases, it may still be difficult for some teens to open up and talk to their parents about some things, and as a parent, the best we can do is to encourage them to find an adult they can trust and confide in, even if it is not us. It may be difficult to accept that we are on the outside of this particular aspect of our child's life, but the most important thing is that they can find an outlet to get honest answers to their questions, express concerns or fears, and feel like they have a safe place in case of any issues. Some people we can suggest our teens seek out for this type of relationship would be a trusted aunt or uncle, an adult sibling, a guidance counselor at school, or even a therapist if they are open to it. Having a close relationship with our child does not mean they will be comfortable to talk about every detail of their life with us, and there is no need to get offended or pass judgment on our child for wanting to keep some things private from their parents. It is simply another way for teens to assert their independence.

Keeping an eye on our teenager's mental health is also important, and can help identify the reason for negative behaviors that cause us to lose patience with them at times. If there is a sudden change in the way they are acting, we should talk to them in a non-confrontational way and express that we care for them and want to make sure they don't need help navigating a difficult situation. Teenagers can experience depression, burnout, substance abuse, anxiety, eating disorders, and many other mental health issues brought on by immense pressure, stress, or just a fear of what lies ahead when they make the next transition into adulthood. Be willing to seek outside help, if necessary, to help teens manage these issues, and do not become angry or judgmental with them at this time. The most important thing for parents to do if they identify any of these bigger concerns is to focus on being a support system and providing unconditional love to their child. Allow your child to share with you on their own terms as well, don't try to play detective by prying into the areas of their life they want to keep to themselves. Avoid invading their privacy and betraying their trust. If there are concerns and you feel it is necessary to monitor their cell phone use or social media interactions, then be honest and discuss your concerns with your teenager.

The relationship between parent and child can be delicate, and if the balance of trust and care is off, it can push your teen away, causing them to distance themselves to protect their newfound sense of independence. If you are struggling to communicate in a meaningful way, try to arrange to spend some quality time with your teen doing something you both enjoy. You can let them pick the activity if it makes them feel more involved or even just more inclined to agree to commit to spending a day with their parents instead of their friends. Listen to your child when they are willing to share with you and don't ask questions that require specific and detailed answers. Teenagers will communicate when they feel comfortable enough to do so and will share the information that they want you to have. The best way to learn more about what your teen is going through is to spend time together and share details of your own life with them as well. Teenagers can present many challenges and push parents to their limits on more than one occasion. However, we can take the time to learn to better manage our anger and pass those skills on to our teens resulting in a much calmer, happier household. The reward at the end of this difficult season of parenthood is being able to accompany our children through the next chapter of their lives and support them as they become adults.

CONCLUSION

Taking steps to maintain the bond and relationship with our children is going to be the number one tool throughout their entire childhood that will enable us to show them empathy and compassion. When we better understand the challenges our children are facing and the emotions they are experiencing, it is much easier to relate to them and gauge not only how we should respond but how they need us to respond. Being a calm parent is all about meeting the needs of everyone involved to the best of our ability. Making sure we are taking care of ourselves and our children is going to help us better respond in a calm, patient manner. Throughout the years we spend raising our children, there will be plenty of opportunities to have some amazing experiences and treasured moments together. Letting go of anger and negative emotions as much as possible will allow us to focus more on what truly matters and enjoy the time we have with our children while they are still young. Along with some of the less helpful advice, I'm sure you have been told by many other parents that you have to just enjoy them while they are little because the time flies by much too fast. Parents can get caught up in the constant need to be perfect and raise a perfect child and lose sight of the fact that every moment spent angry is time they don't get back with their children. Being mindful of the fact that our roles within our children's lives will change and we won't always be their number one source of love and care can help many people take a step back from their emotions to refocus on nurturing the bond with our children, even in the face of adversity.

The relationship between parent and child is going to be complex and imperfect. One thing that most parents can agree on, regardless of their approach, is that they want to provide their child with fond memories of their childhood while also being confident that they have equipped them to care for themselves as they go out on their own to face the world. There is no right or wrong way to help guide your child through the many challenges of growing up, and every child fits in differently within their family dynamic. The trick is to use the different parenting styles to your advantage, creating an approach that fits your family and ensures that we provide our children with the knowledge and confidence they need to become emotionally healthy, unique, independent members of society. Applying the techniques that work for us is only one factor in becoming emotionally healthy, well-rounded, and a generally calmer, more patient parent.

Reminding ourselves that parents are still people who have needs and deserve to be recognized as individuals, not just a mom or dad, is important too. Don't allow yourself to get stuck in a routine that leaves no time to meet your own needs. Self-care allows us to be physically and mentally rested so we can better meet the needs of our children and families. Being a parent does not strip you of your value as a person before you had kids, but it can sometimes feel like that is the case. Be gracious with yourself and consider how you would react to a loved one coming to you to express their frustration with themselves when they made a mistake or failed to meet their goals. Offering yourself the same level of compassion and forgiveness can help silence the internal monologue that allows us to feed into our negative emotions, causing more anger and frustration.

Keep your expectations realistic and try to balance them with the fact that while we are parents, we are still human. Accepting that both parents and children are fallible will help us to choose a more patient and gentle approach with our children, and we should try to provide ourselves with that same courtesy. When we experience anger and other negative emotions, it is not as simple as just deciding to turn them off and be better. It takes hard work and dedication to change the way we allow our emotions to affect us. It will require active engagement and practice to learn how to better take back control when our emotions begin to overwhelm us, but it is entirely within our power to use the techniques and resources that are available to us to mitigate our anger when it is rearing its head.

Being a good parent comes down to providing our children with the love and guidance they need to grow into adults we are proud of, and more so, we want our children to become people who take pride in themselves. Throughout this eBook, there has been a lot of information, and one of the major takeaways for parenting children of all age groups is to make sure we are modeling the behavior we want them to demonstrate. This does not mean that we must control our emotions at all times or even try to give the impression that we are perfect people. That is not realistic and will only set our children up to fail. The aspiration for us as parents is to show our children that there are going to be times when we make mistakes and bad choices and that it is ok as long as we accept the consequences, apologize to those we may have affected, and are willing to learn from these experiences. Providing our children with a loving space to explore the world around them as they grow into their own unique personalities is one of the best gifts we can give them as their parents. Keep in mind that the way we interact with our children when they are younger and rely on us to help them form a sense of self-worth and confidence in their abilities will become the framework for how they expect others to treat them when they are entering into new relationships.

Being a parent does not entitle us to the unconditional love of our child, and we must make every effort to act in such a way that is conducive to the development and maintenance of a strong bond with our children. Do not conduct yourself in a way that will require an unreasonable request for our child's forgiveness later on. Measure the response you take with your child as they look to you for the guidance they need. Remind yourself every day that your child is here because of you and that as a parent, you owe them the loving, caring, and stable upbringing that every child deserves. Our children don't actually owe us anything, and their love and respect are things that we must earn and cherish. Managing our anger to become more patient and calm as a parent will indisputably benefit the whole family and allow for more time to be spent on the important things that we want to look back on as we grow older. Follow your intuition and think of your child as someone who, with the right guidance, will become your equal and not someone who is inferior because they are our child. Do not allow your emotions to cloud your ability to view your child for the unique and amazing person that they are. Seek to be the pillar of strength for your child throughout the struggles they face and hold them up when they falter. There is no way to know if our children are ready to stand on their own when the time comes but by taking steps to become the calm and patient parents that our children deserve, we are able to guarantee that they will have somewhere to land if necessary.

A parent will never stop being a parent regardless of their child's age, and applying the skills we have learned will help solidify the bond we have with our children, which is ultimately the goal of every parent. It is never just about being less angry or more patient; it is about being connected to our children in a meaningful way. Consider the impact your words and actions may have on your child's desire to include you in their life and the value you place on being a part of their own story and what your role may be. Everything we do as parents is leading up to the moment that we eventually have to let them go off on their own. Managing our emotions can make that moment a celebration we share with our child and not a realization of regret and time wasted being angry over the little things. The time to build and improve the relationship you have with your child is now. The emotions we experience are very real, and the effort to regain control can be a tedious process but being able to help forge the path you will walk with your child as they grow is worth every ounce of energy we put in.

REFERENCES

Abundant Mama LLC. (2020, June 9). *How to Be a Calm Parent (and Stop Yelling all the time!)*. Abundant Mama. https://www.abundantmama.com/how-to-be-a-calm-parent/

Ages & Stages. (n.d.). HealthyChildren.Org. Retrieved August 5, 2020, from https://www.healthychildren.org/English/ages-stages/Pages/default.aspx

Anger and anger management for parents. (2020, June 22). Raising Children Network. https://raisingchildren.net.au/guides/first-1000-days/looking-after-yourself/anger-management-for-parents

By GoodTherapy.org Staff. (2018, June 16). *When Parents Clash: Managing Differences in Parenting Style*. GoodTherapy.Org Therapy Blog. https://www.goodtherapy.org/

blog/when-parents-clash-managing-differences-in-parenting-style-0616187

Child Development: Ages and Stages. (2020, July 22). CHOC Children's. https://www.choc.org/primary-care/ages-stages/

ControllingYourAngerAsAParent. (n.d.). Www.Pregnancybirthbaby.Org.Au. Retrieved August 4, 2020, from https://www.pregnancybirthbaby.org.au/controlling-your-anger-as-a-parent

Dealing with Anger: Types of Anger – Your Life Counts. (n.d.). Yourlifecounts.Org. Retrieved August 4, 2020, from https://yourlifecounts.org/learning-center/aggression/dealing-with-anger-types-of-anger/

Emotional Intelligence. (n.d.). Www.Psychologytoday.Com. Retrieved August 6, 2020, from https://www.psychologytoday.com/us/basics/emotional-intelligence

Emotional Intelligence: Developing Strong "People Skills." (n.d.). Mind Tools. Retrieved August 5, 2020, from https://www.mindtools.com/pages/article/newCDV_59.htm

Family Health Team. (2019, August 16). *5 Realistic Ways to Practice Self-Care as a Parent.* Health Essentials from Cleveland Clinic. https://health.clevelandclinic.org/5-realistic-ways-to-practice-self-care-as-a-parent/

Foley, M. M. (2019, July 23). *11 Tips for Becoming a Peaceful and Calm Parent*. Child Development Institute. https://childdevelopmentinfo.com/parenting/11-tips-for-becoming-a-peaceful-and-calm-parent/#gs.cpdza8

How Different Styles of Parenting Impact Children. (n.d.-a). Verywell Mind. Retrieved August 6, 2020, from https://www.verywellmind.com/parenting-styles-2795072

How Different Styles of Parenting Impact Children. (n.d.-b). Verywell Mind. Retrieved August 5, 2020, from https://www.verywellmind.com/parenting-styles-2795072

How to stay calm – the ultimate guide for parents. (2019, October 24). The Montessori Notebook. https://www.themontessorinotebook.com/stay-calm/

Infants & Toddlers | Attachment Parenting International. (n.d.). Www.Attachmentparenting.Org. Retrieved August 5, 2020, from https://www.attachmentparenting.org/parentingtopics/infants-toddlers

Kadane, L. (2017, April 5). *When parents have different parenting styles*. Today's Parent. https://www.todaysparent.com/family/different-parenting-styles/

Lamott, A. (1995). *Bird by Bird: Some Instructions on Writing and Life* (1st ed.). Anchor.

Leyba, E. L. (2020, June 10). *25 self-care ideas for exhausted parents*. Motherly. https://www.mother.ly/life/25-self-care-ideas-for-exhausted-parents

M. (n.d.). *Improving Emotional Intelligence (EQ) - HelpGuide.org*. Www.Helpguide.Org. Retrieved August 5, 2020, from https://www.helpguide.org/articles/mental-health/emotional-intelligence-eq.htm

Managing Anger. (2019). Www.Psychologytoday.Com. https://www.psychologytoday.com/ca/blog/imperfect-spirituality/201903/managing-anger-and-other-big-emotions

Munson, J. (n.d.). *Losing Your Temper with Your Child or Teen? 8 Steps to Stay in Control*. Empowering Parents. Retrieved August 5, 2020, from https://www.empoweringparents.com/article/losing-your-temper-with-your-child-8-steps-to-help-you-stay-in-control/

National Center on Shaken Baby Syndrome. (n.d.). *What is the Period of Purple Crying*. Purplecrying.Info. Retrieved August 13, 2020, from http://purplecrying.info/what-is-the-period-of-purple-crying.php

Parenting Style Affect Your Kids. (n.d.). Www.Psychologytoday.Com. Retrieved August 5, 2020, from https://www.psychologytoday.com/us/blog/cutting-edge-leadership/201410/how-does-your-parenting-style-affect-your-kids

Parenting Styles. (n.d.). Www.Apa.Org. Retrieved August 4, 2020, from https://www.apa.org/act/resources/fact-sheets/parenting-styles

Parents Day Off. (2017). Washington Post. https://www.washingtonpost.com/gdpr-consent/?next_url=https%3a%2f%2fwww.washingtonpost.com%2flifestyle%2fon-parenting%2fin-defense-of-a-parents-day-off%2f2017%2f01%2f23%2f270ffafc-d8f2-11e6-b8b2-cb5164beba6b_story.html

Plas-Plooij, F. X., Plooij, F. X., Rijt, H., & van de Rijt, H. (2019). *The Wonder Weeks: A Stress-Free Guide to Your Baby's Behavior (6th Edition)*. Amsterdam University Press.

Practice Positive Discipline | Attachment Parenting International. (n.d.). Www.Attachmentparenting.Org. Retrieved August 6, 2020, from https://www.attachmentparenting.org/principles/discipline

Rn, S. M., & Frcp, S. W. M. (2001). *The Attachment Parenting Book : A Commonsense Guide to Understanding and Nurturing Your Baby* (Illustrated ed.). Little, Brown Spark.

Saving Your Relationship When You Disagree on Parenting. (n.d.). Verywell Family. Retrieved August 5,

2020, from https://www.verywellfamily.com/tips-dont-agree-on-parenting-4107372

Self-Care for Parents — PEPS. (n.d.). Www.Peps.Org. Retrieved August 5, 2020, from https://www.peps.org/ParentResources/by-topic/self-care/self-care-for-parents

Stonelake, M. (2016, April 27). *7 Strategies for Empathic Discipline*. Empathic Parenting Counseling. https://empathicparentingcounseling.com/5-strategies-for-empathic-discipline/

Strategies Controlling Anger. (n.d.). Www.Apa.Org. Retrieved August 4, 2020, from https://www.apa.org/topics/strategies-controlling-anger

The Benefits and Dangers Highly Empathic Parenting. (n.d.). Www.Psychologytoday.Com. Retrieved August 4, 2020, from https://www.psychologytoday.com/us/blog/feeling-it/201604/the-benefits-and-dangers-highly-empathic-parenting

The science of attachment parenting. (n.d.). Www.Parentingscience.Com. Retrieved August 5, 2020, from https://www.parentingscience.com/attachment-parenting.html

Understanding Anger and Anger Management. (n.d.). Ontario.Cmha.Ca. Retrieved August 4, 2020, from https://

ontario.cmha.ca/documents/understanding-anger-and-anger-management/

Vassar, G. (2011, March 1). *Do You Know Your Anger Triggers?* Lakeside. https://lakesidelink.com/blog/lakeside/do-you-know-your-anger-triggers/

Why Parents Really Get Angry At Their Kids. (n.d.). Www.Psychologytoday.Com. Retrieved August 5, 2020, from https://www.psychologytoday.com/ca/blog/anger-in-the-age-entitlement/201508/why-parents-really-get-angry-their-kids

Why we get so angry at our kids and what we can do about it. (n.d.). Www.Ahaparenting.Com. Retrieved August 4, 2020, from https://www.ahaparenting.com/parenting-tools/positive-discipline/handling-anger

Printed in Great Britain
by Amazon